Welcome

Fly fishing is a sport that anyone, from any walk of life, can enjoy; however, it does take a little longer to master than most types of angling.

It has many different faces, each one a challenge and certainly different from the next, while no species on any continent is out of bounds for the fly fisher.

From the modest river brown trout that can be enticed with a well-presented dry fly or nymph, to aggressive sea bass that have an appetite for sandeels and other small fish, fly anglers have the ability to target them all.

Fish eat 'stuff', we tie flies to represent 'stuff', and that's why we are so effective – we've the ability to tailor our approach to suit any given situation and no other form of fishing allows this tailoring to the extent that fly fishing can.

This is the reason why our sport is so popular the world over; we have the ability to 'dip our toes' where other angling styles fail to tread.

Other forms of fishing seem blinkered, other anglers are often fishing 'blind', if you like, and it's very much a case of chuck it out and hope something pulls back with other styles.

Fly anglers can often see and target their quarry with a well-presented fly; the skill level is far greater, the feeling of satisfaction multiplied tenfold. We've no bait nor lures that we can rely on. Instead, with no more than a well-selected concoction of fur and feather

tied to a hook, we can fool the most finicky of fish!

In this book we bring together some of the best and most skillful fly fishers this county has to offer, in order to furnish other anglers with the skills required to help them become a more complete angler. No matter what type of fly fishing you are into, we have it covered.

As an avid fly fisher, I am privileged to get out on the bank regularly with many of the top names in the sport, and although the venues, tactics and anglers are often very different, the best minds in the game share several key attributes.

The most obvious is an overwhelming desire to succeed in what it is they are doing. Their focus, when they are on the water, is total. They are able to shut out other distractions and concentrate solely on what they are doing, to ensure that when they get 'in the groove' they are able make the most of it.

In the very best anglers, this goes further – they know that if they can modify or tweak a certain method they will have an edge over others.

This, I think, is where the aspiring angler can learn a lesson from their peers. How many times have you come off the water thinking: "If only I had tried a different line, fished a little slower, moved around more often or just thought about things that little bit longer?" The only way that you can guarantee an improvement in your fishing is to leave as little to chance as

possible, and with this book we hope to have all eventualities covered.

It is packed full of imaginative features by anglers who are at the top of their game, bringing you up-to-the-minute advice from the very pinnacle of the sport.

We have tried to cover every discipline of fly fishing, so, whatever you are into, there should be something in here for you.

Enjoy the read, and learn from the masters of the art. With their advice, and your hard work, you WILL become a better angler!

Steve Cullen, Editor

A Fly Fisher's Year *Contents*

Published by David Hall Publishing Ltd. The advertisements and editorial content of this publication are the copyright of David Hall Publishing Ltd and may not be quoted, copied or reproduced without prior permission of the publisher.
Copyright © 2013

Compiled and edited by **Steve Cullen**
Layout and design by **Nicola Howe**
Sub edited by **David Haynes**
Reprographics by **Derek Mooney and Adam Mason**

Greenwell's *glory*

The original dressing is taken from the classic 'A Dictionary Of Trout Flies' by Courtney Williams.

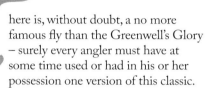

here is, without doubt, a no more famous fly than the Greenwell's Glory – surely every angler must have at some time used or had in his or her possession one version of this classic.

While best known and most frequently used as a dry fly, the winged wet is also famous in its own right.

Conceived and developed by Canon William Greenwell of Durham, the original was actually dressed by the then well-known and now-famous professional fly dresser James Wright of Tweedside, and between them they developed what is arguably the most famous dry fly of all.

The original dressing was devised in May, 1854, for use on the River Tweed at Sprouston. Walk down the same beat of the Tweed today early in the season and I bet you come across at least one angler using a Greenwell's Glory.

At times, there is still no more deadly a pattern than a correctly-dressed Greenwell for both trout and grayling; even sea trout at times!

William Greenwell died in 1918 at the age of 97. He would no doubt be impressed that the fly he invented is still in popular use today.

The Greenwell's Glory is commonly accepted as an imitation of the large dark olive. However, smaller sizes have also proved themselves during various olive hatches, including the blue-winged olive and the like.

While a very effective imitation, as with most flies of this quality, it is also a first-class searching pattern.

Use it even when no hatch is evident. Not only that, it can be successfully used from boat and bank on lakes, rivers and streams.

FISHING TIPS

The dry fly is a classic. Upstream on a light tippet, covering rising fish in the traditional manner, is deadly more often than not. I have found that the wings will quickly split with this style of fly – but the fish don't seem to mind in the least!

A modern parachute version will work well on tricky fish but the classic pattern takes some beating. If you have time to tie them, I would suggest that you tie both.

Wet-fly-style, down and across and with a spider or winged version works a treat in the early season. Even large, educated fish will fall for a well-presented pattern. Remember to feed an upstream mend into the cast to ensure good drift of the fly and to prevent drag.

VARIATIONS

Greenwell's Spider

Rib: Gold wire (optional)
Body: Yellow silk
Hackle: Coch-Y-Bonddu

Wet Greenwell's

Rib: Gold wire (optional)
Wing: Dyed starling
Body: Yellow silk
Hackle: Coch-Y-Bonddu

1 Fix the hook in the vice and ensure that the shank is horizontal to your work surface.

6 Now wind the wire rib up the body in neat, open turns.

11 Tie in the hackle and trim the excess; take care to trim only the waste and not the hackle!

TYING THE GREENWELL'S GLORY

Rib: Gold wire (optional) **Tail:** Greenwell's cock hackle fibres **Wing:** Inside of a blackbird's wing (dyed starling is now the accepted substitute. Try a Veniard stockist) **Body:** Yellow silk **Hackle:** Coch-Y-Bonddu.
The yellow silk should be well smeared with cobbler's wax to achieve a dull, olive colour. A frequently popular addition from the past was a gold wire rib.

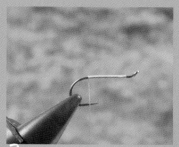

2 Start the silk 4mm from the eye and work in close-touching turns to the rear of the hook.

3 Tie in the tail and the fine gold wire; try and keep the underbody as neat as possible.

4 Treat the silk to get the required colour. If you are struggling, a coloured pen will do.

5 Form the body with neat, close-touching turns of silk. Take your time to achieve a neat body.

7 Tie in the cock hackle with the concave side facing the shank of the hook.

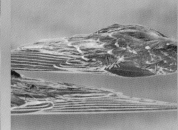

8 Cut two matching wing slips from a dyed starling wing. A blackbird wing is a no-no!

9 Fix the wings into position with a pinch and loop. Ensure they are fixed securely.

10 Start to wind the hackle behind the wing, moving it forward and carefully past the wing.

12 Finish off with three half-hitches and secure your work with some clear varnish.

« Unlike the conventional duo method, this new way of fishing allows you to slide your dry fly up and down the leader. You can now fish water of any depth and flow without having to set up a whole new leader! Genius!

The Dynamic *Duo*

Ben Bangham reveals a stunningly effective new method that will revolutionise the way you fish a river… forever!

*t*here aren't many new fishing gizmos or fads that can impress me, let alone totally change the way I fish. So it came as a mighty shock to discover that a friend of mine had devised a method of fishing the duo that is not only very simple – like all brilliant inventions – but tremendously effective.

I love fishing the duo – a two-in-one method where a nymph is suspended beneath a dry fly – but it does have its drawbacks. Picture yourself fishing the method along a nice stretch of river. You come to a fabulous pool where you can see big grayling feeding, but immediately encounter a problem. Because you have been fishing the shallow water in the race from the pool your duo is set too shallow to fish for these grayling properly.

By the time you have set it up to fish deeper there is every possibility that you may have missed your chance. So imagine being able to adjust your duo depth INSTANTLY, giving you the opportunity to fish for the specimens without losing the valuable – and vital – time it takes to retie the setup. It is something that has always been considered impossible… until now!

UTTER GENIUS

When my pal Stewart Tanner came into my shop and told me that he had a fantastic new way to fish the duo that would improve my fishing I wasn't too convinced, although he was adamant that it worked. Fishing the duo is a method that is very dear to me and one that I really enjoy, so despite my apprehensions I was prepared to listen to what Stewart had to say and my ears really pricked up when he kept insisting that I would be able to change the depth I wanted to fish at in the blink of an eye.

He took me out to his car to show me this 'genius invention' in all its glory! It looked just like a normal New Zealand-style duo setup, where you tie the dropper onto the bend of the dry-fly hook so that they align, greatly reducing the chances of tangling. It wasn't until I inspected it closer that I realised that the leader WASN'T ATTACHED to the hook at all and was, in fact, coming out of the fly!

With a swift tug of the fly Stewart then increased the distance between the nymph and the dry by about two feet. Now that did impress me, because I could instantly see the setup had the potential to be something pretty special.

This is a very clever way of fishing the duo and is essentially a totally movable dry fly, which means it can be set at various distances from the nymph, which in turn means that you can work the nymph at different depths without having to retie the whole setup.

It's very simple and works by passing a length of leader through a bit of foam that is tied into the fly. The grip that the foam exerts onto the leader means that under pressure it can be moved, but stays firmly in place if there is little or no pressure on it – enough to hook a fish properly when it takes the dry fly. Once hooked, though, it will then slide down to the bottom of the leader as the fish is being played, allowing the angler to exert the right amount of pressure to bring the fish to the net.

RIVER ANTON

In a bid to explain exactly how this great innovative tactic works I felt I felt a trip to the River Anton – a tributary of the world-famous Test – just below Andover, in Hampshire, was needed. This stretch of running water is a stunning and true crystal-clear chalkstream full of grayling and trout, and perfect to demonstrate the effectiveness of a movable duo. It's

A stunning little River Anton brown, wild as they come and surprisingly easy to catch with the dynamic duo.

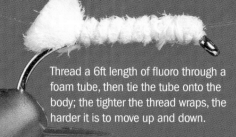

CREATING THE FLY

Thread a 6ft length of fluoro through a foam tube, then tie the tube onto the body; the tighter the thread wraps, the harder it is to move up and down.

Tying it is really very simple if you have the right tools for the job. You will need a pin, a bit of cylindrical foam, a couple of micro rings and three to four feet of 6lb fluorocarbon.

First of all, cut a piece of foam to fit the hook that you are using. The foam cylinders used in tying the bodies of Daddy-Longlegs seem to be best. Put the pin through the centre of the foam and then take it out, leaving a sufficient hole to pass the fluorocarbon through without too much trouble.

Start to tie the fly and tie the foam onto the length of the hook shank, leaving the majority of the fluorocarbon behind the fly and just a small tag coming out of the front. Then tie your dry as normal. The type of fly is up to you but the best ones are big and buoyant; Caddis and Klinkhamers seem to work well. Once you have finished the fly tie on a micro ring to each end of the fluorocarbon. The length of fluorocarbon represents the amount that you can move the fly to adjust the depth.

One of my initial worries was that the thickness of the 6lb fluoro would be enough to put the fish off from taking the dry, but to be honest I haven't seen much evidence of this at all. The thickness of the fluoro is actually kind of key for the whole thing to work. If it's too thin then, because of the way that it's tied, the whole thing can pivot a bit too much and get tangled. It's also very useful in that if you get snagged you will tend to just lose the nymph rather than both flies.

The setup doesn't last forever and there will come a point when you need to change the whole thing; however, if you tie it correctly it's very robust and will last for a long time and catch you a huge amount of fish. Generally the dry fly will fall to bits or the hook will become too blunt to hook fish.

Shallow glides are notoriously difficult to catch in, but by changing the nymph on the point to a dry fly the fish never seemed spooked.

a typical stretch of river with rapids, glides and pools to go at, with plenty of depth variation.

Normally you have to set the duo up at a different depth for each stretch, which wastes a lot of tippet material but more importantly is time-consuming. The use of the adjustable duo means you can set up for all of the water that you are going to cover.

My general approach is to put about two feet of tippet onto the bottom micro ring so you can fish water with a depth of between two to six feet. The top micro ring goes onto a very short tapered leader of about four feet, making the overall length 10 feet. This will cover most situations and if you need it longer or shorter to cover more extreme depth changes then, with the use of the micro ring, it's still really simple to change.

QUICK CHANGE OF DEPTH

I started on a nice smooth glide with a good few grayling that were glued to the bottom, and that's where they stayed despite trying a large variety

of flies over them. After a frustrating hour I moved upstream to the top of the glide where, fishing at about six feet, I hooked up on the bottom almost straightaway. I moved the fly down the leader to make it work shallower until the fly stopped snagging and it was fishing at the perfect depth in the new bit of river.

Fish could be seen but because of a sudden drop in temperature the day before, conditions needed to warm up before they would have a go.

Still, at least I could easily fish all the parts of the river effectively with the same method without too much changing. After a frustrating time at the top of the glide I moved into a small weir pool where I immediately set the duo to its deepest setting, cast it into the pool and had a cracker of a fish around the 1lb mark, and very welcome it was. After a few more drifts through the pool I moved fairly quickly up to the shallower bits above the weir, as I thought that they might have warmed up a bit more to induce the fish to feed. I did land a couple of fish but they were brownies; not my target species, but it

Once you're happy with the tension, go ahead and tie your fly!

did show the method was working like a charm.

DISCO SHRIMP DOES IT AGAIN

By early afternoon the water was starting to warm up and, as a consequence, the grayling started feeding. Every now and then one would move off station to feed on a passing nymph and then slowly drift back to its lie. With the depth adjusted I started to fish and immediately had a grayling inhale my Disco Shrimp – the start of a run of nice fish that lasted nearly an hour. I could have had more but I kept on moving to different bits of water to ensure that I was constantly varying the depth and demonstrating the effectiveness of the 'dynamic duo'. I managed to catch on it in all depths of water, which, over the session, saved me a huge amount of time of retying my leader.

DOUBLE DRY

At one point in the afternoon there was a little hatch of olives that the fish responded to. Now you may think that I would need to change leaders to get these fish as, due to the size of the indicator fly, the fish were unlikely to mistake it for an olive. However, I have encountered this situation before and all you need to do is move the indicator fly to the top of the leader, put your desired dry fly on the point and hey presto… double dry!

I took a lovely grayling of just over 1lb on the dry during a very short session just before an extremely cold rainstorm, but the surface activity didn't last long so the nymph went back on. I fished a few more areas and caught there too!

This breakthrough in fishing the duo has revolutionised the way I fish the tactic and while I am as sceptical as the next angler – probably more – when it comes to new methods this is one that I really do urge you to try.

It's very rare that you find something that has such a profound effect on how you tackle a water and changes your opinion on a method you've been comfortable and reliant on for so many years. Once you've tried the dynamic duo, you too will never fish the same way again!

Fishing his amazingly effective Disco Shrimp deep down under the dry, Ben took this cracking grayling of just under 2lb, one of his best of the day.

Flood conditions above Ridge Pool, River Moy. The
worm fishers are out in force, but there is another way...

High-Water *Heads*

There's no need to break out the spinning rod when faced with the raging
torrent of a salmon river. By adapting tackle and technique, the fly angler has
every chance of connecting with a silver springer.

Picture this: you've been looking
forward to your week's spring salmon
fishing since Christmas. Mid-March
can be a great time to connect with a
spanking silver fish and you just know
that your luck's in… or maybe not!

Forty-eight hours of rain have
fallen in the region before your
arrival and the beat you are to spend
the next week on would currently
scare the most masochistic of white-
water rafters. While the anglers
brave enough to still venture to
the riverbank, instead of consoling
themselves in a bar, are launching
pieces of metalwork across the river
with stout spinning rods, you just wish
there was a way you could fish a fly.

There is, but it ain't gonna be pretty!

Early season with a big water and
big current means a big fly. True,
not all of the time, but it's safe to
say that nine times out of 10 you'll
be looking at long tubes that need
to be fished deep. Salmon in river
conditions such as those mentioned
aren't up for using stacks of precious
energy by attempting to lie in intense
flows. Instead, they will more often
than not be found in the seams of
current – that is, between the fast and
slower water.

This narrow band of water could be
right under your feet, or it could be
three-quarters of the distance across
the river. This means that to fish

effectively, versatility is the key. Short
and long-distance casts must be both
achievable and effectively fished, and
once the line hits the water it must
sink quickly enough to ensure that
the fly swings slowly right in front of
the fish.

Shooting heads are becoming
increasingly popular in UK and Irish
salmon fishing – testament to the
success of the Scandinavian pioneers
of the techniques involved. While
complete kits of the lines containing
a variety of densities allow a versatile
approach, the core of salmon anglers
will most likely stick to their favourite
Spey lines when it comes to floating
and sink-tip methods.

Where the fast-sinking heads really prove an advantage over conventional lines is in chucking the 'big stuff' stupid distances, and searching at depth. With a head far shorter than a conventional Spey line, the shooting head attached to a fine-diameter running line can almost be fished as a lead weight on a mono main line.

The thin, running line provides minimum resistance both in the air and in the water. This allows vast distances to be reached when shooting the line and minimises the effect of strong currents dragging the line away from the lies too quickly.

When casting, the running line should be stripped in and held in as large coils as possible, with the rear of the head positioned a few inches outside the rod tip prior to casting.

Foxford Rocks Fishery on the Moy holds numbers of fish, even in water levels this high.

True, the necessity of stripping and handling large amounts of running line prior to and during the cast can be a pain, but overall the pros outweigh the cons.

WHICH SHOOTING HEAD?

A number of line manufacturers produce ready-made heads to suit this style of fishing. One of the companies with the longest pedigrees, its payroll reads like a who's who of Scandinavian salmon angling, is Guideline. A large range is available to choose from and it's simple enough to pick the ideal line.

The heads are designed to be

Grip the running line tightly between the upper and lower hands and against the reel frame.

trimmed to length, depending on rod length. As a guide, 43 feet is pretty much ideal for a 15ft rod, more for a longer rod, less for a shorter one – experiment, but go easy with the scissors!

Teeny T-series sink-tip lines are also popular, especially when fished in extremely fast, powerful water. The T-500, sinking at nine inches per second, is suited to a 15ft 10-wt rod, although the extra length of the saltwater version can be an advantage for distance casting.

Alternatively, make your own. Short pieces of high-density line won't vary too much performance-wise, so even

factory-second lines will do the job. What you need is a double-taper line two weights heavier than the rating of your rod. Therefore, for a 15ft 10-wt, we need a double-taper 12, high-density line.

There are a number of methods for attaching your leader to the front end and the running line to the rear end of the head.

The three additional inches at either end of the head (see diagram below), allow you to strip the coating from the line and form a loop from the core. This is by far the strongest join, essential if you want to land that 30-pounder in a heavy flood. The loop

CUTTING A SHOOTING HEAD FROM A DOUBLE-TAPER LINE

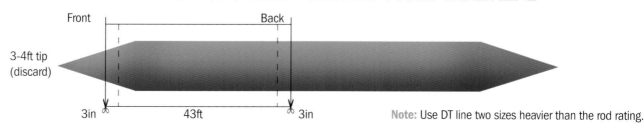

Front | Back

3-4ft tip (discard)

3in | 43ft | 3in

Note: Use DT line two sizes heavier than the rod rating.

Patrick 'Papy' Ford tails a gleaming springer from Foxford Rocks Fishery – who needs a spinning rod anyway?

can be formed by doubling-up the core, whipping over it with tying thread and then glueing, or by simply tying a loop in it as you would a mono leader.

RUNNING LINES

There are two main forms of running line for shooting heads: PVC and flat-beam/oval monofilament. They both have advantages and disadvantages and,

BOTTLE TUBE
Tube: Loop Bottle Tube, large
Wing (1): Veniard Glo-Brite No3 **Wing (2):** Yellow arctic fox **Wing (3):** Six strands of pearl Krystal Flash **Wing (4):** Orange Icelandic sheep **Wing (5):** Black arctic fox **Hackle:** Orange guinea fowl

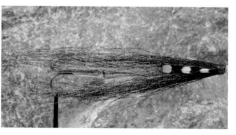

GOLD WILLIE GUNN
Tube: Two to three inches, aluminium or copper
Body: Gold Mylar tubing
Wing (1): Orange and yellow buck tail, mixed
Wing (2): Black buck tail
Cheeks: Jungle cock

CASCADE TUBE
Tube: Two to three inches, aluminium or copper
Body (1): Flat silver tinsel **Body (2):** Black floss
Rib: Oval silver tinsel **Tail:** Orange and yellow buck tail, mixed. Three strands of pearl Krystal Flash **Wing:** Black squirrel. Three strands of black Krystal Flash **Hackle (1):** Yellow Schlappen
Hackle (2): Orange Schlappen

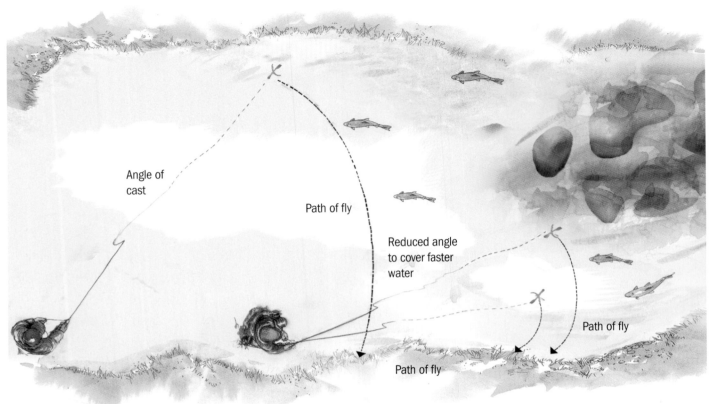

Keeping control of the fly's speed is vital for success – fish it deep and slow. Therefore, in strong flows, cast at a shallow angle, covering the seams in the current.

Long wings are the norm when fishing heavy water, and by tying on plastic tubes mobility is increased.

as such, the keen angler will benefit from carrying both.

When casting extreme distance, minimum resistance from your running line is vital. Flat-beamed monofilament offers this advantage but takes a little more handling skill to master. Monofilament can be prone to memory and therefore tangling, so before fishing take time to give the whole running line a good stretch.

Being thin and pretty darned slippery, this type of running line can be tricky to hang on to when casting. By gripping the line tightly against the reel with both the upper and lower hands, slipping and therefore botched casts can be kept to a minimum. Using this running line really is an advantage when hitting massive distances and, with an overhead cast, 50 yards plus is achievable.

If extreme distance isn't so important, or you wish to Spey cast with your shooting head and would like a setup that is easier to manage, go for a PVC running line. The slightly thicker diameter gives the system more of a conventional Spey line 'feel', enabling more control when setting up the D-loop of the cast. PVC running lines generally have less memory, which aids handling and reduces the likelihood of tangles. Most of the well-known fly-line companies produce a range of running lines that are just the job.

TACKLE FOR VERY HIGH WATER

Rod: 14ft 9-wt to 16ft 11/12-wt, depending on river size

Lines: Shooting heads appropriate for rod. Types II, IV, VI, X should cover most eventualities

Leader: Three to six feet, depending on fly size; shorter for larger flies, or to fish deeper, and 17lb breaking strain minimum

'FLY FISHING HOLIDAY BREAKS'

THREE DAYS FLY FISHING £180 per 2 Anglers
ADDITIONAL DAYS £50 per 2 Anglers

Three days or more motorboat fishing on our four prestigious fisheries, transferable to all four waters, all within 40 minutes drive. Fishing includes the fishery bag limits each day plus catch and release. There is a 10% discount on any tackle you buy at the Lodges during your stay.

SEVEN DAYS BANK FISHING AT A SPECIAL PRICE
£132 per angler transferable to all four waters

Visit our website for more details:

www.anglianwater.co.uk/leisure

TELEPHONE THE FISHING LODGE OF YOUR CHOICE TO BOOK YOUR HOLIDAY

Prices shown current in 2013

CONTACT
Rutland Water
01780 686441
Grafham Water
01480 810531
Pitsford Water
01604 781350
Ravensthorpe
01604 770875

love every drop
anglianwater

Hawthorn *Havoc!*

John Pearson and six-time English National Rivers Champion John Tyzack extol the fish-catching properties of the hawthorn fly.

There are times when a few good, all-round fly patterns will see you through a season. If you spend more than a couple of days a year on the riverbank, the chances are that at some time you'll have bumped into flies from the order Ephemeroptera (the upwing or mayfly-shaped flies).

Even if there hasn't been a hatch of olives for several days the trout often retain a 'search image' that triggers a feeding response to our imitations… so in the absence of any observations to the contrary a nymph or dry Olive is often a good place to start.

There are times, however, when Mother Nature throws you a curve ball. The hawthorn fly (Bibio marci) can turn the fishing on its head, and if you're not prepared when you get to the bank (on stillwaters as well as rivers) you could miss out on some of the most exciting and frantic sport of the season.

Emergence takes place any time from mid-April to early May, earning the hawthorn fly its alternative name of St Mark's fly (owing to its regular appearance around St Mark's Day, on April 25th). If you're not out and fishing during this time you'll not get another chance until next year, as the adult stage of the hawthorn fly only lasts for this very short period.

Unlike many flies imitated by fly fishers the hawthorn is terrestrial in origin. For those of you who have heard the word 'terrestrial' but were too afraid to ask, in fly fishing terms a terrestrial is any creature (usually an insect) whose lifecycle takes place entirely on or over land. The only reason a terrestrial insect ends up in the water is by accident – an accident that most terrestrial insects are ill equipped to handle.

The hawthorn fly is one of the poorest fliers you'll see – think of a bumble bee having a bad day – but it's an even worse swimmer! Even the mildest breeze is enough to make them crash land all over the water. This is bad news for the hawthorn but good news for the trout, and even better news for us fly fishers!

ONE IS ALL YOU NEED

The only stage we need to worry about imitating is the adult stage.

When observing the hawthorn fly at rest, the most pronounced features are its back legs, which are almost grasshopper-like in proportion to its body. The legs become even more apparent when in flight and hang down behind the fly, making identification in the field a fairly easy job, even for a beginner.

We'd love to tell you that the tying in this article is the result of hours of observation, experimentation and study. The truth is a quick look in JT's fly box led us to the conclusion that someone else had already done the hard work.

Most artificials leave us thinking: "There's room for improvement there," but JT's Hawthorn hits the nail on the head perfectly.

When we look at the natural insect we can see that the key points to consider, whether tying or buying a Hawthorn fly, are:

They're completely black; the rear legs are very pronounced; the abdomen is slim and two-thirds of the body length; the thorax is very pronounced; and if viewed from below, the wings are almost hidden by the abdomen.

All of these features are quite clearly covered in JT's simple tying.

Also, males are around 10mm in length and have large eyes, making the head about the same size as the thorax; females are larger (up to 15mm) but with a much smaller head.

TROUT'S-EYE VIEW

It doesn't take the trout long to realise that these leggy black things are an easy meal.

Any river angler worth his salt can (or can at least aspire to) land a dry fly like thistledown, with barely a ripple. When fishing Hawthorn flies, or any other terrestrial pattern for that matter, a splash on the surface can be just the trigger that the trout is looking out for – so the delicate dry approach needs to become more like the natural fly's catastrophic splashdown.

Add to this a pronounced pair of dangling back legs (another key trigger point) and you'll find it hard to fail if the fish are 'on the hawthorns'.

JT HAWTHORN

Hook: Maruto D04, size 14
Thread: SemperFli nano-silk, black
Abdomen: Micro chenille, black
Thorax: SemperFli UV Straggle String, black
Legs: Two knotted pheasant-tail fibres per leg, dyed black
Wing: Polypropylene floating yarn, white
Hackle: Black cock

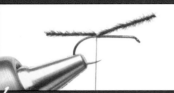

1 Run the thread on the hook and secure the chenille at the rear. The length should be the same as the hook shank. Trim.

2 Now secure the UV at the rear and wind on in touching turns. Stop behind the eye and cut the waste.

3 Tie in the polypropylene yarn to form the wing and trim to size. It should be the same length as the body.

4 Add the knotted pheasant tail; one set of legs on either side of the hook shank. Remove the waste.

5 Tie in the hackle by the stem and wind round the shank three times. Secure and tidy with thread wraps. Varnish.

John Pearson »
took this large River Wye rainbow from a tricky lie after it was spotted making splashy rises to natural hawthorns.

"How many hawthorn patterns do we need, boys?" One, apparently.

awthorn flies have always been a bit of an enigma to me. For several years after setting out on my fly fishing journey I never even saw one. Looking back, the emergence of this particular species of insect must have always coincided with my absence from the riverbank. As a young teenager living a long way from my nearest trout river, fishing days were few and far between. The period of hawthorn fly emergence is short and was easy to miss.

I then progressed to a loosely intermediate awareness of hawthorns. This was when I found that there were occasional late-spring days when the large dark olives were no longer hatching in their previous numbers, and the fish seemed content to take a fairly big black fly.

Walk past a hawthorn tree in full flower and you'll see thousands of them. With the extra-long pair of hind legs hanging down below the abdomen they're unmistakable. I guess I just never made the connection in the early days between these awkward landlubbers and the big black things that the fish would take at around the same time of year.

I now have a definitive imitation, which is my go-to Hawthorn pattern. I don't have a plan B as I've never needed one – if the fish are taking hawthorns then you need the JT Hawthorn.

I've had many an exciting day with this pattern, but the one that sticks in my mind is last April on the Derbyshire Wye. JP and I were on the upper beats of Cressbrook & Litton Fly Fishers' water.

We were weren't really on the lookout for rising fish, but there are certain types of rise forms that no red-blooded angler can ignore!

I can't believe just how hard and viciously trout will hit hawthorn flies. After all, as JP has already said, they don't swim well and they should represent an easy meal that fish can merely sip down with a minimum of fuss… but they don't. These rises are full-on surface attacks that send spray showering everywhere and get the angler's heart racing.

We were approaching a lovely looking pool on a gradual right-hand

bend. Both banks were swathed in hawthorn trees in full flower. It was picture-postcard stuff! The downstream wind ruffled the surface of the river and there were regular, huge, noisy and energetic rises.

We decided to set the rod up and try for these fish. My usual 12ft leader was constructed, comprising a 9ft Hardy copolymer tapered leader with a 5X point; this time water knotted to a 3ft tippet of 6X Stroft, which has a 0.12mm diameter. (Remember: think diameters not breaking strains!)

On went the JT Hawthorn and then we had the usual 'fight' as to who had the first cast. Possession is nine-tenths of the law, and since I'd made up the leader and tied on the fly I pulled rank. I consoled JP with the words that I'd probably get one straightaway so he wouldn't have to wait very long.

I made a series of nice casts from a good position downstream of the rising fish. The fly sat perfectly in the surface film (not on it, remember it's a drowning terrestrial) and the trout completely ignored it.

Hawthorn time follows hot on the heels of Large Dark Olive time, and I'd spent the past few weeks landing olive patterns gently in front of fish… but olives don't tend to crash land! My presentation was just too good (yes, this is possible!). Changing the casting plane and stopping the rod later on the forward cast allowed me to make a slight 'plop' with the fly as it landed on the water, and this brought instant results. A nice plump ½lb rainbow tried its best to shed the hook with a series of runs and leaps that wouldn't have disgraced a fish twice its size. The wild rainbows here are turbocharged.

JP was quickly in on the act with a brownie that had some fantastic markings on the adipose and caudal fins. The action came thick and fast up the pool, and while the fish kept rising we kept catching. It wasn't rocket science; we just had to get the fly to 'crash' a foot or so upstream of a feeding fish and bingo!

Towards the top of the pool, with JP on the rod, we spotted a much better fish still gulping down the hawthorns greedily tight under the far bank,

but with that slightly less hurried approach so common among the bigger fish of the river. It was going to need a good cast as the fish had a great lie (another indication of what is likely to be a bigger-than-average fish is where it chooses to feed). This one was under the far bank with bushes overhanging, but to make matters worse there was little room for a back cast…

He delivered the perfect cast first time. The trout took and all hell let loose. The fish dived for the roots first of all, but side strain averted that little ploy. Then it went aerial with a series of jumps and splashdowns that all threatened the hook-hold. JP won this little battle after a couple of heart-stopping minutes for him, and he slid the net under a lovely rainbow.

We'd had about 40 minutes of nonstop hawthorn action, culminating in a lovely fish, and it was time to continue our search for filming locations up the river.

Meanwhile, get a few of these Hawthorns tied up and have some fun with the St Mark's Fly…

The Sulk

Hook: Short Shank Special, sizes 8 and 10 **Thread:** Black
Body: UV Gold, lime green Micro Straggle **Tail:** Black marabou **Wing:** Black and
chartreuse barred marabou **Hackle:** Black hen

Black and green is a lethal combo and anyone who fishes for trout knows that. However, most flies tend to follow the same path. This one, with the addition of barred marabou, sticks out a bit more than the usual offerings.

It'll work best fished deep down on a sinking line for recent stock fish and resident trout, especially browns.

Originally designed as a mini-lure, it can also be tied a lot larger and perhaps with the addition of a bead head for small-water applications.

1 Fix the hook into the vice and wind on the tying thread to create a body before attaching the marabou, then trim to size.

3 Wind the Straggle up the shank of the hook, keeping the turns nice and close so as not to see the black underbody.

5 Take a lovely soft hen hackle and attach at the head, then wind around the shank three or four times.

2 Take a length of the Straggle and attach to the hook. Run it along the shank to keep the body nice and even.

4 Secure the Straggle, trim the waste and then attach the barred marabou wing, the same length as the tail.

6 Secure the hackle, trim waste and tidy the head, before whip finishing and varnishing.

Klinkhamer
Special

Often described as a modern dry fly, this king of all-rounders has been around longer than you may think. The Klinkhamer was originally designed as a grayling pattern but is equally effective for trout on all waters.

Hans van Klinken's inspiration for his now world-famous Klinkhamer pattern came in 1984 from the stomach of a grayling. To be more precise, it came from a large caseless caddis larva found inside the grayling's stomach.

The perfectly curved shape for the bug was created from a large Partridge grub hook and the next objective was finding out how to encourage it to float. A poly-yarn wing and bushy parachute hackle proved to be the answer. Hans found that, when the wing and hackle were treated with floatant, the fly sat perfectly in the surface film with the abdomen hanging in the water. This proved deadly for trout and grayling feeding on emerging caddis pupae, and so the Klinkhamer Special was born.

Since its conception, the Klinkhamer Special and its multitude of variants have been used to imitate many insects, from emerging sedges and midges to upwing flies as well as terrestrials. This versatility makes it one of the best 'searching' patterns going. For those days when you're not sure what the fish are taking or when you're on the move and need a reliable all-rounder to search the water, you can count on the Klinkhamer Special.

This is a simple pattern to tie, so long as you can form a decent parachute hackle! Hans' own unique method ensures optimum flotation of the pattern as well as providing a robust finish – essential to stop it falling apart after so many fish!

The colour of the fly can be varied to suit the imitation of a huge range of bugs, although the general rule is 'abdomen light, thorax dark'. Tie this fly in a wide range of sizes, from a seemingly unlikely 8 down to as small as you dare. This will enable you to fish confidently in a hatch of more or less any insect – even when you don't know what the insect is!

One problem that 90 per cent of fly anglers experience when fishing dry flies, especially small ones, is in spotting them on the water. Have no fear! One of the great design features of this pattern is that you can make it as visible as you like, with little or no effect on the fish. Simply tie the wing post long and bushy, or alternatively tie it using a bright-coloured yarn. The important part to the fish is that the abdomen hangs under the surface and the hackle gives an impression of legs on the surface film.

FISHING TIPS

RIVERS

When tying Klinkhamers for fishing fast-flowing rivers, make sure to be generous with your turns of hackle. By also adding a brightly coloured wing post, you'll end up with a fly that floats like a cork and is easy to spot, even in white water.

Hans van Klinken advocates fishing the pattern downstream. This is not often used in the UK when dry-fly fishing but is a technique that every river angler should master. It presents the fly to the fish before the leader and the fly line enter the fish's view.

Another deadly technique, and one favoured by the England team, is to fish a tiny nymph underneath a Klinkhamer. Simply make sure the hackle and wing post are well treated with floatant and it'll support even small Gold Heads – a deadly 'searching' setup.

STILLWATERS

The main food form for trout on most stillwaters is midge pupae or buzzers. The curved shape of the Klinkhamer makes it a pretty much perfect imitation of the hatching midge and, therefore, you should dress the pattern in colours to suit. These can then be fished singly on a long, tapered leader or in a team with other emerger-type patterns, such as Hoppers or Shuttlecocks.

Those anglers who refuse to fish a strike indicator, due to the likeness to float fishing (we won't go there yet again!), will find a passable alternative in the Klinkhamer. Tie them large, size 8, and bushy with a highly visible wing post. As with the river setup, this can then be treated with a floatant and is easily buoyant enough to support two or even three buzzer patterns.

1 Form a single layer of thread along the hook shank. Tie a strand of poly-yarn in towards the front.

6 Tie in two or three strands of peacock herl and wind the thread to the eye of the hook.

11 Using your fine thread, tie off the hackle onto the wing post. Very carefully, whip finish and varnish underneath the parachute.

VARIATIONS

Hi-Viz Klinkhamer

Hook: Curved buzzer, sizes 10 to 24
Body: Tan Veniard Squirrel Dub **Thorax:** Dark brown Veniard Squirrel Dub **Hackle:** Grizzly olive cock **Wing post:** Veniard Glo-Brite Multi-Yarn No4

Caddis Klinkhamer

Hook: Curved buzzer, sizes 8 to 18
Body: Tan dubbing **Thorax:** Peacock herl
Hackle: Cree cock **Wing post:** White poly-yarn

Black Buzzer Klinkhamer

Hook: Curved buzzer, sizes 10 to 16
Body: Black thread **Thorax:** Peacock herl
Hackle: Black cock
Wing post: White poly-yarn

TYING THE KLINKHAMER SPECIAL

2 Wind back towards the bend, tying over the excess poly-yarn to ensure a neat body.

3 Tie in the hackle so that it lies alongside the yarn. Turn around the hackle and wing post twice.

4 Wind back as far round the bend as possible and apply a small amount of dubbing to the thread.

5 Wind the dubbing up to just before the wing post, keeping the body as slim as possible.

7 Twist the peacock herl strands and wind them both sides of the wing post to form a dark, chunky thorax. Whip finish and varnish.

8 Take the fly and rotate it a full 90 degrees in the vice.

9 Carefully, attach the fine thread using several overlapping turns and create a solid base by winding around the wing post.

10 Wind your hackle with the shiny side facing downward. Use five turns for small flies and seven turns for large flies.

12 Cut the wing to a concave shape and trim off any hackles that point downward.

CATCH MORE ON THE FLY...

Available on the App Store

Available on Google play

Available on kindle fire

Also available for the following:

Available on BlackBerry

Available on PC & Mac

at pocketmags.com

Grab your favourite fishing reads on the go!

Available in single issues or save £££s with a variety of subscription offers – see app for details.

To get the required app, search 'Total FlyFisher' in your app store or at pocketmags.com

PLUS!
These great fishing titles are also available

Mighty *Nice!*

Surface lure fishing for sea trout is often thought of
as a last-resort tactic. We travel to the far southwest
to demonstrate why it should always be part of your

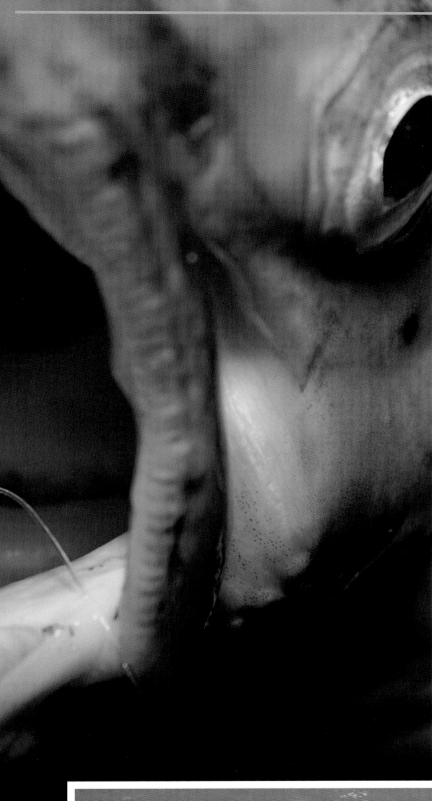

f there was a dictionary definition for surface lures it would be a buoyant fly designed to catch sea trout by causing a wake on the water surface when retrieved.

Hugh Falkus first wrote about modern surface lure fishing, discussing in detail the techniques and patterns required to trick sea trout into taking on very dark nights. It is certainly a fact that very dark, warm nights produce the best results but this is true for most sea trouting, not just surface lures.

For some reason, the River Fowey in Cornwall produces more than its fair share of fish to the surface lure each year. Perhaps it is the mild weather that makes the fish more inclined to rise to a waking fly, or that the topography of the river lends itself more to this style of fishing than others.

WATER TO LOOK FOR

Ideal surface lure water is, in general, slow and shallow. Smooth, unbroken pool tails and shallow canal-like glides are what you should be looking for. Although some writers have advocated the use of surface lures in very deep water, on the Fowey best results seem to come in water of less than two feet deep.

If you haven't fished a particular river before, it makes no sense at all to turn up in the dark and try and fumble your way around, imagining likely holding areas. Always walk the river during daylight hours. This is for two reasons, the most important being safety. As you will be wading for much of your fishing, checking the pools out will give you a good idea of the deep spots!

The second reason is to locate groups of fish to target later in the night. I am a firm believer that confidence is the most important key to success and by finding a group of fish during the day, confidence will be high when making those first casts in the dark.

What many people don't realise is that on very shallow stretches the fish will often go unnoticed during the day. You need to look out for undercut banks alongside these shallows and, more often than not, the fish will be tucked away, almost out of sight. Look more closely and you will often see a tail or two poking out from under the bank – a bit like an ostrich burying its head in the sand!

This is what you're looking for! A nice pod of fish lying in a perfect surface lure pool.

Perfect surface lure water.

Local angler Graham Bray has fished the Fowey for decades and almost exclusively uses surface lures at night. Graham is not one to wait until it is late on only the darkest nights in midsummer and often finds success from early dusk, even at the start of the season in April!

As far as tackle goes, you must use gear that suits the river. That sounds obvious I suppose but much of the Fowey is heavily overgrown and short, accurate casts are all that are required.

Rods sold for sea trout fishing are often long, slow-actioned models designed for easy roll casting and 'cushioning' when hooking fish. In tight situations on small rivers, it is often vital to position casts underneath overhanging vegetation. Therefore a short, fast-actioned rod is a real help – enabling precise, tight loops to be shot under the trees.

To allow for the lack of 'cushioning' that the rod tip provides, holding the rod tip two to three feet above the surface while retrieving provides a little

slack line – allowing the fish to turn after taking.

The ideal length would therefore be 8ft 6in to 9ft 6in for a 6/7-wt line – floating of course.

As far as flies go, we have two standard patterns and a sneaky extra. The formula is for a very buoyant, bulbous body tied on a large single hook, with a small treble attached via monofilament or wire extending beyond the bend.

Even with this nasty-looking ironmongery, the surface lure suffers from more short-taking bites than any other fly.

The two most common materials used for the body are deer hair and Plastazote. These large creations certainly do the job and the lures will float all night. However, you will often find that many fish will be missed or pricked and lost – solid takes can be a rarity.

Sea trout will take a surface lure from any angle and therefore the larger the target, the more likely it is that the

fish will miss the hooks.

On the Fowey, Graham Bray and others prefer to use a smaller lure, with the minimum amount of 'bulk' possible. This gives the fish a small target to hit and therefore it is more likely to engulf the lot!

Another theory for missed fish can be simply down to the solid and bulky properties of spun deer hair and Plastazote – these materials don't crush when hit by a fish. Sea trout often hit the lures at lightning pace and many seem to 'bounce off' the bulkier fly.

With this in mind, Graham and his friends have come up with a pattern that not only floats like a cork, providing the all-essential wake, but it's very slim and soft, enabling the fish to 'get a grip'.

Another advantage of the pattern is that, being very light indeed, it can be comfortably and accurately cast using the 6-wt tackle advocated on the Fowey – try it with a 2in Plastazote job!

The fly is tied on long-shanked

SUPER SEDGE
Hook: Partridge YK12ST size 8 or 10
Body: Two to four black CDC hackles
Wing: Virtual Nymph Realistic Caddis-Wing
Head: Strip of black Plastazote, folded over **Eyes:** Red Veniard epoxy eyes, 3mm

MIGHTY MOUSE
Hook (1): Low-water salmon size 6
Hook (2): Treble size 14 attached via 25lb mono
Body: Veniard black Booby Eye (Plastazote cylinder), trimmed to shape **Tail:** Black buck tail or squirrel with two strands of Krystal Flash

MOUSE
Hook (1): Low-water salmon size 6
Hook (2): Partridge outpoint treble size 14 attached via 25lb mono **Body:** Deer hair, spun and clipped to shape **Tail:** Olive buck tail or squirrel with two strands of Krystal Flash

A daytime recce is highly recommended and essential when fishing unknown water.

Partridge sedge hooks that, due to their pronounced bend and relatively heavy wire, hang well down in the water – offering maximum contact to the fish. The all-important wings provide much of the buoyancy and, due to their V-shape, a fantastic wake on the water.

They are made from printed silk sheeting, sold by Virtual Nymph as Realistic Caddis-Wings. By soaking the wings in Gink or a similar floatant, they lie flat on the surface and the odd snappy false cast is all that is required to keep them floating all night. With a wound CDC body and small Plastazote head (don't forget the eyes!), the deadly Super Sedge is complete.

There are two main ways of fishing the Mouse. We'll start with the primary set-up, because the second is a neat trick to fool short-taking fish. The main set-up would therefore be a 9ft 6-wt rod with a 6-wt floating line. When fishing a very narrow stretch it can be a good idea to use a 7-wt line with the same rod as it helps to load the rod with only a short length of line.

If possible, use a 9ft tapered fluorocarbon leader, cut down from the butt to about seven feet long. This will help turn over the fly and, as fluorocarbon sinks, avoid any unwanted wake from the leader. Having said that, it always pays to degrease any leader with a sinkant – just to make sure. Alternatively, a simple leader made of five feet of 10lb and two feet of 8lb will do the trick.

Having carefully approached your chosen pool, make sure that it is dark enough to start fishing.

Roll casting is vital on much of the Fowey.

Travel light – you won't want to be laden with kit when wading and walking.

Make sure you carry a few spare flies – you WILL lose some!

You'll often read 'wait until the bats start to fly' and 'until you can't make out the colour of the grass' but to be honest, it isn't an exact science and as long as you're struggling to tie a fly on without a torch, it's probably dark enough!

When you start fishing, take your time and concentrate. Stomping into the river and covering the water as quickly as possible won't do you any favours and is more likely to involve flies lost in trees, frustration and spooked fish. Fish the water close to you first. As soon as dusk falls the fish tend to move around the pool, often then resting in the tail. By making short, square casts you may well be covering fish that you would have spooked had you fished the 'prime' water first.

On the Fowey, Graham has found that the upstream cast outfishes all others. By casting at 30 degrees upstream of square, a lure can be fished underneath overhanging trees more effectively – covering both the fish lying tight to the bank as well as those in more open water. Retrieves can vary, but the old favourite has to be a medium figure of eight. This keeps the lure waking at a constant pace and has proved to be most effective.

As the fishing is done in the dark, takes can obviously be hard to read – learn to use your ears rather than your eyes! What Graham has found is that the more aggressively a fish goes for the fly, the less likely that a solid hook-up will result.

You will often get huge, nerve-shattering crashes of white water as a fish haphazardly lunges at the fly, or large swirls as the fish comes short. The most positive take, according to Graham, is when you simply hear the fish 'gulp' the fly down. This can sound like a quiet 'slurping' sound and is usually (fingers crossed!) followed by the rod nearly being wrenched from your grip.

The sneaky second method comes into play if you find that, although you are moving a lot of fish, you fail to hook or even prick any. In a similar way to big-game fishing for tuna or swordfish, the surface lure can be used as a 'teaser' to attract the fish's attention.

Try attaching the Mouse to a

The Super Sedge will often catch small sea trout.

Howzat! A cracking early-season six-pounder on a Mouse.

dropper, about 12 inches from the point fly – a 'standard' size 10 or 12 wet fly such as a Silver Stoat's Tail. The inquisitive fish will often come to investigate the waking fly, snatching the point fly as it spots it – deadly!

When playing fish in such a small river, you have to expect fireworks. As there are very few deep pools and as much of your surface lure fishing will be done in the shallows, there's only two ways that the fish can run – upstream or downstream.

If you hook anything over even 2lb on little rivers like the Fowey you are in for one hell of a fight. Sea trout have to be the most 'mental' fish when attached to a line and this is where knowledge of the beat is essential.

Often, the only way to keep up with a running fish is to get in the water and chase it – just make sure you know where you are going, safely! The trick to all sea trout fishing is to persevere – experiment on your own river and do not limit yourself to fishing in only 'perfect' conditions or at specific points during the night.

Graham has taken fish on bright, moonlit nights with a bitterly-cold chill in the air – sea trout will break the rules whenever they can!

TEASER RIG

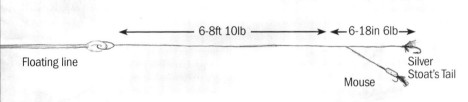

Floating line | ←— 6-8ft 10lb —→ | ←6-18in 6lb→ | Silver Stoat's Tail | Mouse

FISHING THE MOUSE

Desert Island *flies*

England international Rob Sosbe reveals the fly patterns he couldn't live without.

BLACK DIAWL BACH

The Black Diawl Bach would have to be one of the most productive patterns that I have in my fly box. It manages to catch me fish right through the season.

What more can you ask for?

I often find that this cracking little pattern scores well early on in the season when fish are readily taking buzzers, then again during the summer months. It seems that the black colour stands out well in the all-too-often coloured waters during algal blooms. The fly's profile represents a great variety of aquatic species. When the pin fry make an appearance it often takes its fair share of resident fish; these fish are not easy to catch and the slim, drab profile makes this pattern a winner.

I can safely say that this is the one fly I would never be without.

Hook: Kamasan B175, size 10 **Thread:** Black
Tail: Black hen **Body:** Black pheasant tail
Rib: Fine silver wire **Throat hackle**: Black hen
Cheeks: Jungle cock

THE CABBAGE

When looking through my lure box – and believe me there's a lot to look at – I often search this pattern out. It is my favourite middle-dropper fly without a doubt. It has accounted for a great deal of fish during competitions and a bigger version of this pattern works a treat from the banks too!

I find that the pattern produces well when fish are feeding on daphnia – in particular the prevalent blooms of the green stuff – and it makes a great alternative to the usual Blobs. When fish are tired of seeing the usual bright creations – orange, pink and yellow –whizzing past them, this colour can often get a response, and not just from recent stockies.

Hook: Wet, size 8 **Thread:** It doesn't matter but I like to experiment with Glo-brite colours! **Tail:** Olive marabou **Body:** Olive Fritz

WOOFTA

This crazy-looking Booby was responsible for the vast majority of my catch during the Spring International. This is where I was lucky enough to become International Champion – one of the most memorable days of my life!

The pattern originated on Lyn Brenig but it travels extremely well. It has caught me fish wherever I've tried it. It'll catch on either a sunk line or midge-tip washing-line style. There are a number of various tyings for the pattern but this is the original and, in my opinion, still the best.

Hook: Kamasan B175, size 10
Thread: Chartreuse Tail: Baby pink marabou
Body: Chartreuse chenille **Wing:** Baby pink marabou **Eyes:** Pink foam

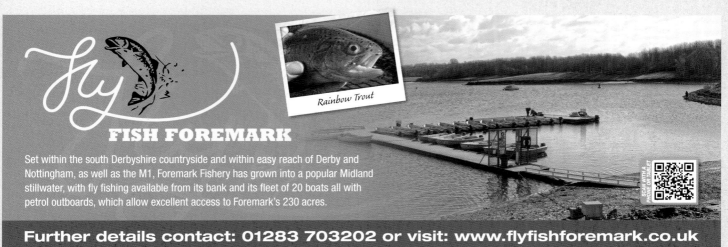

FISH FOREMARK

Set within the south Derbyshire countryside and within easy reach of Derby and Nottingham, as well as the M1, Foremark Fishery has grown into a popular Midland stillwater, with fly fishing available from its bank and its fleet of 20 boats all with petrol outboards, which allow excellent access to Foremark's 230 acres.

Further details contact: 01283 703202 or visit: www.flyfishforemark.co.uk

© Fly Fish Foremark – Derbyshire Fishery is a brand name of Fishery Management (UK) Ltd.

FISH DRAYCOTE

This 600-acre Midlands stillwater is famed for its superb trout and produces the finest buzzer fishing in the Midlands, with its exceptional buzzer hatches. This abundance of food ensures its reputation for large grown-on rainbow and brown trout with fish in excess of 5kg (10lb) caught each year.

Further details contact: 01788 812018 or visit: www.flyfishdraycote.co.uk

© Fly Fish Draycote Water – Stillwater Fishery is a brand name of Fishery Management (UK) Ltd.

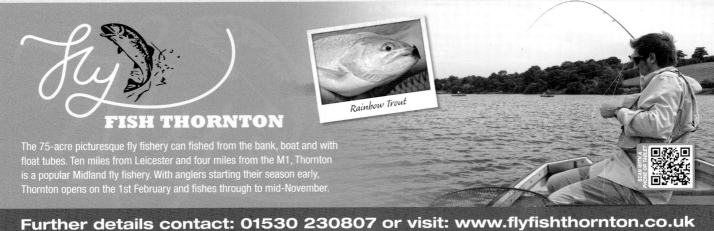

FISH THORNTON

The 75-acre picturesque fly fishery can fished from the bank, boat and with float tubes. Ten miles from Leicester and four miles from the M1, Thornton is a popular Midland fly fishery. With anglers starting their season early, Thornton opens on the 1st February and fishes through to mid-November.

Further details contact: 01530 230807 or visit: www.flyfishthornton.co.uk

© Fly Fish Thornton – Leicestershire Fly Fishery is a brand name of Fishery Management (UK) Ltd.

FISH TUITION

No matter if you're trying fly fishing for the first time or an experienced angler wanting to hone a particular skill, our guides and instructors have been chosen by us to ensure you receive the highest standard of tuition, with Draycote Water offering the ideal reservoir venue.

Courses are available at each of our three fisheries. Day courses take place at Draycote.

www.flyfishtuition.co.uk

© Fly Fish Tuition is a brand name of Fishery Management (UK) Ltd.

FISH STORE

We stock all the major brands and our website is easy to navigate. We have secure online payment and you can link to all our lakes. Check us out now and 'JOIN OUR FLY FISHING COMMUNITY'.

Sales order line: 01788 812018
www.flyfishstore.co.uk

© Fly Fish Store is a brand name of Fishery Management (UK) Ltd.

Charles Jardine's
Troubleshooter

With the help of 'Skateboard' Dave Egginton we see
if we can get Charles Jardine his first carp on the fly.

t was decided that my education should be broadened, well, more 'raised' from my usual and brought into another plane entirely.

It was time I tried something different; to have someone guide me for a change. Also, to try for another species. I thought gudgeon on a fly might be different and fun. Actually, I quite like catching gudgeon; they've saved a slow trotting day on many occasions. But on a fly?

I know that this is all getting a little weird, but stay with me.

'Skateboard' Dave Egginton, the guy who ties all those little bloodworms and damsels and stuff for coarse fish, was the man to help me.

"Forget the gudgeon," Dave said when I called, "I can get you into some big carp!" Now we're talking!

Years previously, when pterodactyls wheeled about the Dorset cliffs, I used to fish for tench on some Kent gravel pits with a fly. It seemed to upset the 'proper' fishers, but what the heck. Actually, the only reason that we upset these guys is because we caught fish. But apart from the odd accidental coarse fish and the odd excursion after pike, that was it.

But carp, now there's a thing. And with Skateboard Dave, too. You only have one life – live it!

GEARING UP FOR THE DAY

N o-one bothered to tell me what to bring, what we would be using, the size of the carp – which, let's face it, can mean anything from a few ounces to 40 or something pounds. I didn't know the type of water, or what flies would work – I knew nothing.

So what does one do in an event like this? Bring everything, that's what!

It was then that I realised the sort of trauma that newcomers must go through. Do I buy this? Do I bring that? And so on – nightmare!

I took just about everything, from a 0-wt-wispy-wand-like-thing, up to a far more robust 10-footer for an 8-wt and every permutation in between, with matching reels of course, and with every line at my disposal, just in case. There was nylon of various diameters. And flies! Heck, I even threw in the salmon and sea trout box. Well, I didn't know, did I?

I could have stocked a shop.

Oh! And a net. I did refrain from putting in the long-handled barbel net. Then there was the short-stay bivvy (the one that they enthusiastically promise you can put up in two minutes and 30 minutes later you are bathed in sweat, littered with bruises and abrasions and using the ribs as offensive weapons! I digress).

I forgot the clothing. They didn't tell me where I'd be fishing. Was I going to wade? Was it deep? Would I be hanging upside down from a tree like a fruit bat? What? Enough. Onward.

Anyway the car was stuffed.

Charles 'I Have Everything But The Kitchen Sink' Jardine.

That will be a gudgeon on a fly then.

THE ARRIVAL

W inding through the Leicester countryside was like something out of a Sir Alfred Munnings 'gypsy' painting (Munnings was – for you heathens – probably our best equestrian artist of the last hundred years) – there was blossom and colour sprinkled over trees, hedges and ditches; bright, glossy-green, velvety fields and sky so blue it looked like a precious stone in a fine ring. Young life was bursting everywhere: there were mares with foals and birds with broods. It was England in her finest summer clothes. Peckleton seemed ideal, no: an idyll.

Skateboard Dave – as the name might suggest – is not the usual vision of fly fishing; he's refreshingly 'untweedy' and as non-trout-trendy (you know: designer base-ball cap, flats, shirt and trousers and so on – the current uniform!) as you could get, but with a welcoming smile as bright as the day and a handshake as warm and welcoming as the sun. I was going to enjoy this.

Then, through the oasis of green it came, a deep growl and high-pitched whine of various engines in states of racing or idleness suggested a rather different scenario. So lads, Mallory Park. Why?

The answer was simple – Roy Marlow's excellent, coarse fishing, match-oriented waters, close to one of our premier motor-racing circuits, offered us just the right introduction to this style of fishing – motorbikes or not!

Dave said, as we discussed the day: "It might be too easy today boys." I can stand 'too easy', I really can.

STUFF THAT LURKS IN THE BOOT – OR NOT

W e drove to the car park and with some trepidation I opened the boot of my car. Dave was astonished. "You carry way too much gear," he said. I wouldn't disagree.

Dave's gear was enlightening. There was an obligatory skateboard of course, a few rods – two I think – and that was it. There were no waders and no 'tackle shops'.

I looked at his multi-sectioned 9ft (it used to be longer, but a previous encounter of a piscine kind had shortened it by a few inches) soft-actioned rod. "I like this because it is the only 3/4-wt rod that I have ever found that has an extension butt, so that I can support the rod when I am playing fish; you'll need it (I liked his confidence!). I have some small Sages and other types of rod for other styles, but this one is perfect for blind margin fishing and at reasonable range for cruising fish," he said.

In the end, I went for a 10ft 4-wt, which seemed to be what was required, matched to a floating line, combined with a normal fly reel with backing. I will come on to this later.

A TERMINAL CASE –
TACKLE ME TO YOUR LEADER

While I am not exactly obsessed with leaders, I do feel that this crucial part of our system is given very small billing; indeed, almost glossed over.

"And leaders?" I queried.

"Oh! in this type of fishing a straight length is sufficient. Now if I am going to fish at range to visible fish…" suggested Dave, "I will use a tapered leader, then it's very important to get good turn over. However, in this instance, you will only need about five feet…"

"Whoa!" I said, "let's stop you there. Five feet! You're kidding, right?"

"Seriously, it's all you need. These fish are not intelligent, especially not at this time of year. They will be, once a few matches have started, but right now you can get close, as long as you keep a low profile and fish almost on top of them."

So five or so feet of 5lb copolymer was attached to the tiny metal ring (I am increasingly getting fond of these!) of my 2ft nylon butt section. Overall leader length with a dropper or two was a massive eight feet.

Now before all you folk think we have gone barmy, there is a great deal of logic in this leader system, as I was to find out.

I had brought waders, and I was going to wear them!

Dave, on the other hand, took the more relaxed route. He wore a pair of red-and-white Vans sneakers, long shorts (if that makes sense), a T-shirt and a very interesting rat-pack style pork-pie hat. It wasn't the usual fly fishing gear, but Dave isn't the usual fly fisher. He also carried everything needed for the day in a flats pack – Dave finds this far more versatile for his various needs than a conventional, multi-pocketed vest. I had the vest and realised the mistake. Too much stuff again – oh well.

Charles auditioning for Brokeback Mountain II.

A lunker under the trees.

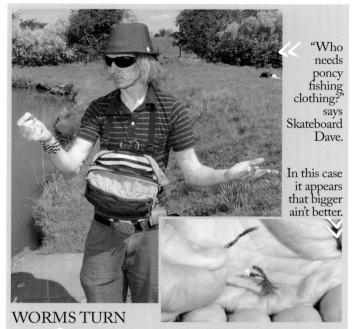

"Who needs poncy fishing clothing?" says Skateboard Dave.

In this case it appears that bigger ain't better.

WORMS TURN

Now for the flies. There was a good proportion of classics and favourites in Dave's fly box: damsels, midges, olive dry flies, little black dry midges and so on. The difference? All were on hooks below a 14, most on 16 to 20 with a fair percentage on smaller, say 22 to 28. Again, it wasn't the usual box, and Dave isn't the usual fly fisher.

"So, what do you recommend Dave?" I queried.

"I have tried a lot of patterns," he replied, "but the best of all, by far, is a bloodworm."

I pulled out an oily worm – a deadly favourite for trout.

"No! Not like that! Way too heavy. No movement. Way too big as well. It will sink past the fish before they have a chance to take it."

"Anything else wrong with it?" I ventured.

"No, apart from that, it's great."

No oily worm for Jardine then.

It transpires that carp, especially if you are fishing blind and in the margins, sort of suck in the fly – a bit like us noisily demolishing a tasty soup I guess. The marabou, Dave reckoned, helped this process and, importantly, the near weightlessness of the pattern allowed the fly to hover, dance and just react in the vicinity of feeding or cruising fish.

What truly surprised me was that Dave then proceeded to place three of these 'weightless' tiny bloodworms on a 5ft leader. How? You might well ask. It was a tight fit.

I opted for a slight variation of one of Steve Cullen's foam pellet imitations as a form of indicator on the top dropper, and bloodworm below. I have to say, Steve, that the imitation is uncannily like the real thing and you have led a very bad life in some parts of Scotland! The pellet, in Skateboard Dave's eyes, was cheating. Purists eh?

I have to admit to initially having massive reservations about doing this feature. But these were gradually dripping away in the wake of increasing confidence that this might actually work.

THE SMALL MATTER OF DOING IT: THE OPERATION IN THE FIELD

*t*he lake was surrounded by trees and was just a little more serene than the whine and roar of racing bikes across the road. We approached over the brow of a high bank and immediately saw carp, lots of carp.

The water looked to be a matter of only a few feet deep at the edges, and beyond this apron of shallow water lay a shelf to deep water, but that seemed to be irrelevant. The shallows were obviously the key areas, although there were a few cruisers carving a wake in the surface out towards the central island. Dave hunkered down along the margins and laid siege. Suddenly I realised why his leaders were so short – takes.

"Use a longer leader," explained Dave, "and you simply never see anything. You have got to see and react to the slightest twitch or tremor on the leader and strike. A short leader registers this immediately. A short leader means fish; a long one, nothing."

As long as you were cautious and stealthy you could almost stand on top of your quarry. You only needed casts of a few yards, sometimes less. You just needed to place the fly in an approximate area of feeding; obviously the nearer the better but essentially that was it. I can do this, I reasoned.

Dave flicked a cast into the very side of the bay from his crouching position and did nothing. "Don't retrieve. Just let the flies get washed around in the feeding turbulence and the subsurface currents work the flies. The only time that you might retrieve is when you are casting at cruising fish. It's classic nymph fishing really," he advised.

Steve and I were transfixed as carp snaked along the margins, stopping periodically to search the bottom for food. All Dave did was to cast and allow the wind to drift the flies into the margins. As we watched hawk-like, a sudden glint of gold flashed to the side and Dave's hand shot skyward; the small wand of a rod immediately hooped over.

First fish, and I was addicted. The fight – a searing run, then that dogged kiting, surface flails, the lot. I wanted this, Steve wanted this, Dave wanted more. This was awesome. Well, we did get more, lots more. An area just by a straggly little bush was my moment. With Dave guiding me, I cast out and just allowed the line to be pulled by the surface current into the margins.

After a spirited battle that lasted a lot longer than expected, the fish finally comes to the net. »

« The face says it all!

Skateboard Dave targeting the margins.

A delighted-looking convert.

Dave's first carp of the day, taken a couple of feet from the edge.

"There are always fish there." Dave whispered. The flies hadn't even settled when a great, rubbery mouth folded around the Cullen floating Pelletus horribellus and sucked the whole thing in. I was so mesmerised I almost forgot to strike – almost. On a 4-wt the fight was indescribable. It was fantastic – you have to do this!

"See. Great isn't it?" Dave said. I was addicted. I had a smile of unbridled joy – and that is exactly what this fishing is – joyous. I also caught properly, on one of Dave's bloodworms. Dave's flies were the key. My patterns, as good as they are, are for trout, so they were just plain wrong for carp. The key was the lightness and the marabou. If a bright bead was needed, then it was a glass bead rather than metal. The patterns had to waft, almost hover, subsurface.

The other crucial factor is striking as soon as you see the fish turn. Miss this and the moment has gone. If we thought there were a lot of carp in the area we had initially dropped into, Roy Marlow's suggestion that we "might like to try the top end as there's a few there" was possibly one of the greatest understatements in history. It was packed with feeding fish. Dave assaulted these like a man possessed.

I asked, casually, how many carp he might expect on a day like this and unhesitatingly he said: "Ooh, about 20 or so. Of course, it gets harder once the matches get under way and the season starts, and not every fishery is like this. You might only get one or two a session on other, harder waters, but if you put the time in, walk the bank and understand the fishes' habits, then you will get the rewards." It was all comforting news, given warmer summers and the fact that great chunks of the trout season are now being burnt out of the calendar.

I did finish by catching (with Steve's dodgy pellet thing) a near double and I have to tell you that, on a 4-wt rod, in among shrubs, trees and bushes, having targeted the fish at close quarters, this branch (sorry pun unintentional!) of the sport has got one very new and vociferous convert.

I should also add that Dave did, in fact, on the day, catch a gudgeon on the fly. I am dubious about carrying out this somewhat bizarre activity. I mean carp, yes, but gudgeon? And there is no way that you would get me on a skateboard. Again, as for the carp, bring them ON!

Even with the natural mayfly
on the water in numbers, this
beautiful brown still picked
out the Pink Thing.

The Odd One Out

Steve Cullen reveals one of his most successful mayfly patterns that you – and the trout – just can't fail to notice.

Mayflies can be found on waters from the top of Scotland to the southern tip of England and, for trout, these tasty morsels must surely be one of the most widespread delicacies to be found in both still and running water.

However, here's the killer. How many of us can say that we've been fortunate enough to fish in one of these legendary hatches?

I'm sure that if the majority of anglers were quizzed they'd all be of the same opinion – that mayflies are only to be found in southern England. Those same anglers would also be of the opinion that chalkstreams are the preserve of these awesome creatures.

It has to be said, of course, that there are plenty of anglers who know better. Still, as our largest upwing, it seems that this fly is relatively inconspicuous.

It could be that people 'in the know' have a river or stillwater to themselves and are loath to give their secret away lightly.

Since moving to England I've been fortunate enough to see quite a few mayfly hatches, and even more fortunate to actually fish during these wonderful times. These hatches are often referred to as 'duffers' fortnight' meaning that the fish are very easy to catch during this time. Well, let me tell you, I'm convinced that this fortnight doesn't exist. It may do on the heavily stocked chalkstreams of the south, but on the wild waters things are somewhat more tricky.

BIG, HARD-TO-CATCH FISH

At first, when these large flies start to hatch, it seems at times that the trout are scared of them! The trout often rise rather clumsily and miss the flies altogether. However, they soon get into the swing of things and with a steady procession coming off the water they can have a whale of a time.

This hatch can often bring up trout that haven't been seen from one year to the next. In Ireland, huge ferox trout, normally at home chasing smaller fish down in the depths, come to the surface to graze on this abundant food source.

It's the same in UK rivers and lakes – the big boys come out to play. Catching them, though, is another matter.

I was asked to go up to Ingbirchworth Reservoir, in South Yorkshire, a few years ago. This is a lovely expanse of water – 60 acres of wild brown trout fishing that's sure to appeal to any sensible fly fisher.

When I was there the hatch was petering out. It was the near the end of June, but looking from the dam wall I could still see brown trout, some with backs as wide as your knee, sipping down the spent flies.

Sadly, I never managed to fish that day – it was just a flying visit – but those anglers who had been fishing assured me that these leviathans were just not interested in anything that was cast to them.

It's this kind of fishing – targeting huge, wild fish that are extremely hard to tempt – that appeals to us. That's why the mayfly is so special.

AND NOW FOR SOMETHING COMPLETELY DIFFERENT...

There are numerous mayfly patterns out there, although many adult, winged versions are dressed in the same colours time and time again – cream, cream and more cream. This coloration is all very well – in all honesty it copies the naturals perfectly – but I'm a tinkerer and about four years ago I thought about trying something a little different, something to make my fly stand out from the rest.

I tied one in pink. You may well ask why I went with pink. Who knows? I do know that game fish seem to love it, though. As yet, no-one has come up with a theory as to why, but they do.

That was my starting point and more or less finishing point. It looked like most shop-bought patterns, well sort of, but it was a completely different colour.

I wanted to get away from the paired-wing nonsense that spins your leader so terribly, too, so I tied it using simple CDC. It cast beautifully and, because it doesn't spin, there's no need to use excessively heavy leaders. Being made up mostly of CDC, it lands nicely on the water.

This fly stands out… boy does it stand out.

A friend of mine who I was fishing with one day said: "Steve, there is no way a trout is going to take that! It looks like a pink ping-pong ball floating down the river."

I had to agree, but the following story shows that this fly does catch trout when more conventional mayfly patterns won't.

A DAY ON THE DERWENT

Last May I was lucky enough to be asked to go and a have a day's fishing on a pristine stretch of The River Derwent in Derbyshire, thanks to the Darley Dale Fly Fishing Club. This is one of the oldest fly fishing clubs, not just in Derbyshire, but in the country.

Gary Turner and I were informed that there were a few mayflies coming off the water but not to expect anything until late afternoon. This wasn't a problem as I'd decided that I was going to fish nymphs in the morning, dipping into some of the 'popply' water in the hope of picking up one or two brownies.

I had never fished the water before but seeing that it was a freestone water I was confident of catching. Gary, on the other hand, had fished the river before and knew of one or two stretches where I could find this type of water. He put me in at the tail of a set of rapids where the water fell away into a small hole around three feet deep.

Fishing two flies on a long leader it was a case of casting upstream, with a few mends in the line, and allowing the flies to fall through the water column into the hole.

Success was instant. The red-coloured sleeve on the braided loop shot forward just as the line came into the slightly slower water. I swept my arm back, lifting the tip of the little 8ft 3-wt rod until I could feel the stabbing fight of a feisty brown trout.

The fight was terrific. In the well-oxygenated water the trout was full of beans, darting this way and that; this was interspersed with some spectacular leaps, sending a showering spray of water droplets over the pool. Despite its spirited little show it was soon netted, the fly was slipped free and the fish returned to the water.

Moving slowly upstream, dropping in to fish these areas proved to be very

It's a large fly but the trout are more than happy to take it.

Even on tricky 'flat' water the trout still rose confidently to the Pink Thing.

rewarding throughout the morning. But as lunch beckoned there were still no signs of the mayflies.

A LONG, SLOW GLIDE

Gary and I moved up to a long glide, the kind of water where any kind of rising fish would stick out like a sore thumb.

We sat and had some lunch; a pork pie and a bar of chocolate washed down with some fizzy juice bought from the Shell garage down the road. As we ate we saw one or two mayflies on the water. This was encouraging, but I turned to Gary and said: "I just can't see it happening, though, there aren't enough flies on the water."

Gary just nodded his head towards the river and, with a smile, said: "You missed that."

I quickly looked towards the water and saw rings spread across the pool. A trout had obviously risen, and up to the mayflies too.

We both set up our rods accordingly, Gary with his shop-bought flies and me with… the Pink Thing.

I offered Gary the chance to try first. He slid slowly deeper into the pool until the water was up around his middle and he was close enough to try for one of the rising trout.

Gary's a good caster and within a few casts his mayfly was drifting towards its target.

I watched from the bank, smiling, convinced that this fish would take.

It ignored his fly. He turned around, looked at me and shrugged his shoulders. He cast again, perfectly. Again it was the same result. The fish just wouldn't come up.

"Change your fly," I shouted over to him.

As he gathered his line in to swap over to another pattern, the trout rose to another mayfly. Gary changed his fly, watched as the trout rose to take another, then cast above it and let the fly drift into the trout's feeding zone… but still nothing!

THE PINK THING

"Have you put that Pink Thing on?" Gary shouted. "You know I have," I told him. "Come on then. I need to see this," was his reply.

We swapped places, and he turned to me saying: "There is no way that fish is going to fall for that!"

I pulled line from my reel,

> ## "JUST AS I THOUGHT THE FLY WAS PAST ITS TARGET, A LARGE, YELLOWY-GOLD HEAD CAME UP AND ENGULFED THE PINK THING."

lengthening until I knew I had enough off to cover this fish and mend my line a few times. I fished the fly on the end of a shop-bought 9ft tapered leader that ended in a 4lb point – nothing fancy.

It wasn't easy with the little 8ft 3-wt but the light line weight meant that I could present a fly with the minimum of disturbance.

"How many casts am I allowed?" I asked Gary. He was sitting on the bank with a 'you've got to be joking' look on his face. "Are you serious? With that thing on the end I'll give you 10!" he exclaimed.

My first two casts weren't the best; I was up to my chest in the water and the fish was further upstream and sitting on the far side of the river.

My third cast was right on the money. By stopping the rod at 12 o'clock on the forward cast the line came back towards me, introducing plenty of slack before it landed, just perfect for drag-free drift.

The fly landed about two yards ahead of the spot where the brownie had been showing. As it drifted slowly downstream, I said to myself: "It's having it."

Just as I thought the fly was past its target and the drag on my line was about to speed the fly away from the area, a large, yellowy-gold head came up and engulfed the Pink Thing. There was no need for me to strike – the current pulling the line, combined with the fish turning down, had more or less set the hook. All I did was sweep my rod to the side and I met with a gratifyingly solid resistance. I had him!

In the deep water it got its head down, its swift powerful lunges taking line from me and heading upstream. I had no choice but to let it do what it wanted. Gary waded into the water beside me shouting: "I can't believe it, I just can't believe it."

"I know, but there's something about this fly. It can work when other conventional patterns don't," was my reply.

The trout, meanwhile, was starting to tire; the short bursts of power were now a lot slower as I put pressure on the fish to move it downstream.

As the trout drew level with us, it treated us to a dramatic leap, its buttery flanks glinting gold in the early afternoon sunlight. Back in the water I could tell it was beaten.

I gently brought it in towards the net, its head out of the water, guiding it to my outstretched hand. The pink thing was visible in his scissors – he was mine.

What a stunning creature the brown trout is. This one wasn't huge, but it didn't have to be, and on light tackle even a 1lb brownie can be more than a handful.

I gently revived it, cradling it in my outstretched hand as it gathered its strength. Within a minute or so it slipped away into the slow-moving current.

I'd proved my point.

Perhaps next time you're faced with tough trout during a mayfly hatch, you should reach for something pink.

THE PINK *thing*

Hook: Scierra Trout extra long, size 10 **Thread:** Pink 6/0 and brown 8/0
Tail: Several strands of black deer hair **Body:** 50/50 mix of Roman Moser Glassfibre dub, orange and Lite Brite sand shrimp
Rib: Four or five pheasant-tail fibres **Wing:** CDC, two red plumes and one light olive

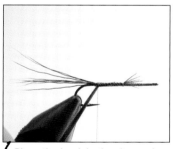

1 Place the hook in the vice and wind on your pink thread, stopping opposite the barb. Tie in a few strands of deer hair, then the pheasant tail, by the tips.

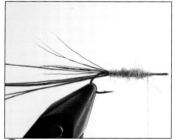

2 Blend your dubbing to create a nicely tapered dubbing rope and wind on up the shank in touching turns. Stop two-thirds of the way up the shank.

3 With hackle pliers, catch the butt section of the pheasant tail and wind it up the shank in open turns, four times. Secure and whip finish.

4 Tie on the brown thread and secure a red CDC feather, by the tips, to the shank. Wind around three times, secure and trim the waste.

5 Now do the same again, this time with the light-olive CDC feather.

6 Take the second red CDC plume and repeat the process, stopping a little before the hook eye. Trim the waste.

7 Strip some fibres from the red CDC plume and dub onto the tying thread, nice and thin.

8 Wrap around the hook shank a few times before stroking the fibres back, whip finishing and adding a touch of varnish.

Desert Island *flies*

The northeast's Paul Davison has represented England at all levels, but is best known as a highly skilled river angler. Here he reveals his top three patterns…

PHEASANT TAIL ORANGE COLLAR

This is probably my top fly of the last five years. The collar acts as a trigger point and in clear water I go down to a size 16. It's an excellent killer fly for grayling, whether it is on rain-fed or spring-fed rivers. I'm a great believer in a fly having some form of trigger point to make it stand out from the natural, and having confidence in a fly is the be all and end all. This fly is the first pattern I reach for each time I fish – it's so versatile it lends itself perfectly to duo-style (dry fly and nymph), double nymph and bugging hard on the bottom with braid. It even works well on stillwaters for spooky fish.

Hook: Tiemco Grub, size 12 to 16 **Bead:** 2mm copper bead **Thread: Black Tail:** Pheasant tail fibres Body: Pheasant tail fibres **Rib:** Copper wire **Collar:** Fire-orange thread

OLIVE STRIPPED QUILL NYMPH

This is a very versatile fly that I usually use in conjunction with the Pheasant Tail Orange Collar. I tend to use copper beads as I personally feel that gold is a little bright. I usually leave the goldheads in the box for days when the river is coloured. Once I have put the stripped quill on, I varnish the body three times, let it dry then the seal's fur is tied in. This makes it very robust and it sinks better. The pearl overcase is my trigger point on this fly. It gives it a lovely glint as it tumbles along the riverbed. This fly has worked for me very well, not just in the UK but all over Europe for trout and grayling.

Hook: Tiemco Grub, size 12 to 18 **Bead:** 2mm to 3mm copper bead **Thread: Black Tail:** Pheasant tail fibres **Body:** Black thread Rib: Open turns of olive stripped quill **Collar:** Light olive seal's fur with a pearl overcase

POLY WING OLIVE

The tying of this fly was given to me by Simon Robinson and has increased my catch rate on dries immensely. It is the first dry fly I reach for at any time of year, and it's very rare I have to try any other dry because this seems to bring the results 99 per cent of the time. It is very simple to tie and covers a multitude of insects. I always fish a single dry and my leader set-up consists of a very fine Orvis Hy-Flote leader with a tippet of 21/2lb of Orvis Mirage. I only grease the first foot behind the fly. I tend to use the bigger sizes in the faster, broken water. The bigger sizes help get the fly down where it matters.

Hook: Czech nymph dry fly, size 14 to 20 **Thread:** Ultra-fine nylon thread **Tail:** Two fibres from a small, nylon paintbrush **Body:** Dark-grey waterproof dubbing **Wing:** Grey poly yarn

Introducing a master class in short range presentation…

The River&Stream rods are produced using only the finest grades of carbon fibre available, delivering unrivalled lightweight blanks with super soft, smooth casting actions. This refined blank delivery allows for ultimate precision when laying flies atop of easily spooked, wild fish…

Lightest Fly Reels in the World*

6'#2   7'#3   7'6"#3   8'#4   8'6"#4   9'#4   9'#5   10'#3   10'#4   10'#5   11'#3   11'#4

*Lightest Aluminium CNC machine cut clicker-drag fly reels on the global market at time of launch: February 2013

from RRP £129.99 - £169.99

Request our new catalogue at www.wychwood-tackle.co.uk

designed in Redditch, England by
Wychwood™

The *Damselfly*

The sign of electric-blue insects flying around the margins of a stillwater is a sure sign of summer. It's also a sure sign of some fantastic, imitative fishing…

A relative of the dragonflies (order Odonata), the damselfly is a favourite summer food item of the stillwater trout. While trout will, at times, take the unmistakable, vivid-blue adult insect, it's the nymph form of the damselfly that is of most interest to them… and, therefore, us, the anglers.

The life cycle begins when, after mating, the female insect lays eggs on a stone or piece of vegetation under the water, which soon hatch to become tiny damselfly larvae. Each nymph may live up to five years in the water before it becomes an adult. During this time it will feed on smaller insects and decaying matter, shedding its hard skin as it increases in size.

The nymph swims by using a slow, but graceful, movement, by flexing

A marabou-tailed damsel imitation is irresistible to summer rainbows.

its long, slim body from side to side, mainly living and hunting around weeded areas.

When it's time for the insect to hatch it will crawl from the water –

usually on a sunny day – onto a weed stem or suchlike. Here the insect sheds its final skin to reveal the adult underneath. Several days prior to this happening the nymph will become more active, having to swim to the surface to breath air. It's at this point that it is particularly susceptible to the marauding trout.

RODS

To extract the most out of fishing damsel patterns you'd be best to go with a proper rod, say a 10ft 7-wt – something with a little bit of poke. The more distance you achieve, the longer the fly is in the water. This means that a lot more fish should, realistically, see it.

For distance work, a fast-actioned rod is the ideal tool for the job. Not

SKINNY DAMSEL
Hook: Standard-shank, size 12
Eyes: Black dumbbell eyes **Tail:** Olive marabou **Body:** Fine olive dubbing **Rib:** Flat pearl tinsel **Thorax:** Fine olive dubbing
Thorax cover: Pheasant tail fibres
Legs: Golden olive partridge

GOLDEN OLIVE LIVING DAMSEL
Hook: Standard-shank, size 12 **Eyes:** Black dumbbell eyes **Tail:** Golden olive marabou, plaited **Thorax:** Golden olive seal's fur
Rib: Oval gold tinsel **Thorax cover:** Pheasant tail fibres **Legs:** Golden olive partridge

BRAIDED BUTT DAMSEL
Hook: Straight-eye, curved hook, size 10
Tail: Braided monofilament, coloured blue and black **Wings:** Grizzle hackle tips
Thorax: Blue dubbing **Wing post:** Blue Ethafoam **Hackle:** Blue grizzle cock

only can you achieve casts to the horizon, but it'll also help you hook fish at range much more effectively than a soft rod.

Don't get too hung up about reaching the horizon, though, because quite often fish can be picked up in and around the margins.

LINES

All manner of lines work for fishing damsels, so make sure you carry everything from a floater to a fast-sinking line.

The best line, however, will probably be either the midge-tip or intermediate line. The reason for these lines being so effective, more so than the others, is the fact that they allow you to retrieve the fly on a level plain, just like the real thing.

If you can keep the pattern at a certain level and bring the fly all the way back to the rod tip this way, then you stand more chance of catching a fish properly that is feeding on damsel nymphs.

Casting along weedy margins will put your Damsel Nymph in the trout's hunting zone!

Try using a jerky figure-of-eight retrieve…

… interspersed with a few 1ft pulls.

What it's all about – a cracking grown-on damsel feeder.

LEADERS AND TIPPETS

If you intend to go at the water with a single fly, then you won't go far wrong with a tapered leader of some description or another. These can make all the difference, especially when you're trying to achieve that little bit more distance. It means that the fly is going to turn over and, effectively, be fishing as soon as it enters the water.

When you are trying to cast far, with a single length of straight-through leader, the fly can sometimes land near the fly line. If this happens then the fly can be taken on the drop without any takes being registered – you don't want this.

Tippets don't need to be fragile, web-like affairs for this kind of fishing. Something like 6lb breaking strain is ideal; you could even up that to 8lb if

there are big fish about.

To get the most from this kind of fishing it can pay dividends to fish a couple of flies. Go for a weighted or gold head fly on the point and an unweighted pattern on a dropper, say, five feet above the point fly. You'll cover more water, and at the same time get an idea of the depth the fish are feeding at.

RETRIEVES

If you are able to see a damsel nymph underwater you'll see that they're very mobile characters. They are aggressive predators and very capable swimmers, swimming from one place to another before resting.

One of the best retrieves is the good old figure-of eight, but not to fast, just slow and steady to mimic the natural insect.

Reed and weed-lined edges are the damselfly's natural habitat.

Proof of the pudding – the stomach contents of a Thornton rainbow reveal a damsel feast!

Another very special retrieve is to execute a 1ft pull, at the same time vibrating the rod tip up and down with your casting hand.

The whole idea is to try to achieve the same undulating movement as the natural insect; this is why long-tailed patterns can be so effective.

LOCATION

Damsels can be found in most still waters and slow-moving waterways, so there is sure to be some in your nearest lake or reservoir.

Weed beds are the number-one locations for damsel nymphs, especially long-stemmed weeds, because the nymphs wait on the underside of leaves to ambush their prey.

Damsels have to crawl out of the water to emerge, so any kind of structure should be paid close attention to. Weed beds, fence posts, trees and boat docks should all be concentrated on. It is from these structures, free from the water, that the nymphs change into adult insects.

Before this change occurs, however, the more clued-up trout can be seen swimming up against these reed beds, knocking the half-emerged damsels back into the water where they are easy pickings.

ADULT DAMSELS

Quite often, although some people will tell you otherwise, trout can really switch on to adult damselflies. If conditions are right, then the trout will actively feed on the egg-laying females.

Dry a suitable imitation – there are plenty out there. Fishing the fly dead drift is often a good tactic. You can also make the fly seem like a struggling insect by giving a quick twitch to your line every now and then.

Make sure you use stout leader again, as these big flies tend to spin when casting. And, remember, you'll often be fishing near weed beds, so don't go too light-handed.

Tummel Trout And The Spent *Spinner*

Howard Croston describes ways to overcome the frustration of spinner-feeding browns on Perthshire's River Tummel. When things look grim, a late start and an accurate cast can be key…

Many anglers new to river fishing frequently arrive nice and early at the river's edge. They look forward to a day's sport on running water; maybe as a change from their normal boat trip to Rutland or local small stillwater where an early start before the hordes arrive can be the best tactic.

However, when venturing out onto large wild rivers such as the Tummel, the best sport is frequently found at the time of day when many anglers new to river fishing are packing up!

This is never truer than during the midsummer doldrums that often see frustrated anglers marching back to the car around lunch time, when the river looks as though there is not a single fish to be had.

Some time later, as the sun finally dips below the horizon, those 'in the know' start to arrive to get down to some serious dry-fly action! While still and fishless in appearance during the day, the same stretch of river at nightfall can resemble a stock pond at feeding time, as fish of all sizes prey heavily on caddis, both ascending and returning, and, of course, spinners.

During the middle of the day, the summer heat can put paid to any action – the trick is to wait until evening.

Tie a short length of fine leader to the bend of a large, visible dry fly and attach your small spinner pattern. This is commonly known as the New Zealand-style method of fishing two flies.

Tools of the trade and a Tummel trout – you don't need to carry the kitchen sink when on the river.

THE SPINNER

The spinner, as anglers know it, is actually the final stage in the life cycle of all the upwings (ephemerids), which, after mating, return 'spent' to the water's surface to perform the final act of propagating the species.

For me, spinner fishing is one of the highlights of the summer season but it can drive many anglers to distraction – why?

Generally, spinners float flush to the water's surface. So, unless you are expecting them, or actively looking for them, they can be nigh on impossible to spot, especially in the

failing light of a summer evening.

When arriving at the river, especially if it is one you have never fished before, always do a little research to help narrow down the possible insect species you may encounter. A bit of rock turning will reveal the likely suspects in nymph form. However, the best plan is to look beneath the leaves on a few bankside trees, because this is where any recently hatched insects will be found.

As a general rule, if I start to see fish rise in a slow, deliberate manner, but cannot see evidence of any adult

flies drifting with the current, I will suspect spinners and start to look a little more closely.

CHALLENGING TIMES

There are a few challenges to fishing successfully with spinners. Without doubt, one of the biggest pitfalls anglers new to river fishing experience is the accurate casting often required to be successful. This is compounded when dealing with a fall of spinners because the fish, during heavy falls, will take up a feeding position quite literally inches or even millimetres below the surface.

This occurs when the available food source of the trout, in this case the spinner, is so abundant that it is more energy effective for the trout to stay up 'on the fin' rather than return to its holding lie beneath the surface. This massively reduces the trout's window of vision, often down to a few inches in diameter. Therefore the fish may never see your offering, unless it drifts right between its eyes.

If you are confident that you have selected the correct shade and size of spinner but get no response, start to question your presentation rather than choice of fly!

One advantage that a fish lying close to the surface presents is that it is quite possible, with a stealthy approach, to get extremely close to a rising fish. This in turn allows you to make a more accurate cast. The small window of vision also allows a short drift over the target and hence more casts.

Try not to give heavily feeding fish too much 'lead' as this is usually a waste of time. Around two feet of drift towards a hard feeder is generally enough. Do, however, allow a little drift behind the fish to prevent spooking it as you lift off the line, and just in case it turns to take your offering after it has passed by – it does happen!

SPOTTING THE RISES

Although a normal single-fly rig is usually the most effective when covering rising fish, many anglers who have less than perfect eyesight may struggle to track a low-floating pattern like a spinner in the evening light. My solution to this, and one

OLIVE SPINNER
Hook: Size 16 straight-eye
Thread: Fine olive **Tail:** Two fibbets, splayed
Body: Olive thread **Thorax:** Fine olive dubbing
Wing: White poly yarn, tied in a figure of eight to lie flat

FIERY BROWN SPINNER
Hook: Size 14 to 16 **Thread:** Fine black
Tail: Two fibbets, splayed **Body:** Black thread
Rib: Fiery brown floss **Thorax:** Fine black
dubbing **Wing:** White poly yarn

FIERY BROWN PARACHUTE
Hook: Size 14 **Thread:** Fine brown
Tail: Two fibbets, splayed **Body:** Fiery brown
dubbing **Rib:** Fine brown thread
Hackle: Grizzle **Wing post:** White poly yarn

TOP TIPS FOR SPINNER FISHING

EQUIPMENT

My trusty 9ft 4-wt is my usual weapon. However, when caenis are on the cards I will drop down to my 3-wt to help cushion light tippets.

My leader will be tapered and at least 12 feet long to achieve a good drag-free drift. You must strike a balance between length of leader and control of the cast, so a bit of experimenting will pay dividends.

APPROACH

Although you can get much closer to a spinner feeder than other rising fish at times, you cannot be careless in your approach. I will often keep low and approach from behind, sometimes on my knees, to gain a tactical advantage. A pair of bicycle kneepads, worn either over or under your waders, can make crawling around on your knees a lot more comfortable.

TACTICS

On hard feeders, a short drift will allow you to make more casts and therefore convert more rises into fish hooked and landed, which prevents you from wasting time drifting your fly over 'dead' water. The one biggest tip that I can pass on to anyone, when it comes to this style of fishing, is accuracy rules!

Another victim of the spinner succumbs to the landing net. This fish was taken in the seam of slack water near the far bank.

that has proved deadly, especially in a fall of tiny spinners like caenis, is to use a two-fly rig.

I will attach a large, dry pattern, like a sedge or large Griffith's Gnat, to the end of my leader and then rig my spinner pattern onto a length of fine nylon, attached New Zealand style to the hook bend. This allows me to track the larger fly and should anything rise behind the 'indicator' pattern I strike. You will also fool the odd fish on the indicator itself, especially towards nightfall, because the fish become slightly less focused on the spinners.

PACK FEEDING

During very heavy falls of spinner, again especially caenis, I have seen the fish form into 'packs' and actively roam around a pool in a group. While there is really no reason for this, it does happen and can provide amazing sport. The fish will often move in a circular route, moving slowly up one side and then turning downstream to start another 'sweep' of the pool.

Do not be tempted to think that there must be a large fall of spinners to use the method. At times of year when spinners are regularly seen, the fish can often accept a spinner fished as a searching pattern. Even if the fish don't actively 'remember' a spinner fall from a few days ago, the vulnerable appearance of a spinner floating prone and helpless in the surface is often too much for a hungry trout.

On the day this feature was shot, many of the fish were lying in a shallow, fast run and were not actively rising. However, they were more than eager to hit a well-presented imitation when given the chance!

A handsome wild brown reluctantly comes to the net, obviously overawed by Howard's tasteful fishing glasses.

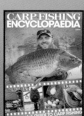
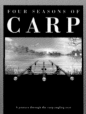
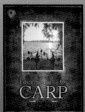

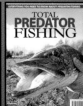

Charles Jardine's *Notebook*

When the trout start to turn their attentions to fry, the stillwater angler can be in for a real treat.

*t*here is, for me, nothing quite like the last-gasp throw of the reservoir dice: hunting fry feeders along the bank.

It remains the ultimate game of cat and mouse and is the essence of mobile fly fishing. Set in a weary world often drably cloaked in mist, brown and grey, the sheer adrenaline-charged moments as fish close in to pounce on hapless victims just fill the senses.

It is a period for the big waters – the Rutlands, Grafhams, Bewls and Pitsfords – many of which are now open until December, and which will offer some of the very finest moments of the fly fishing year. But anglers beware! It is not a period of limit bags and quick-fire fishing. Instead, it is the assiduous assault on one or two marked fish and the narrow-eyed view to a kill that is angling at its rawest edge and, some might say, its very core.

Mind you, the one or two fish that you might catch could be the highlight of the year. Everyone has the idea that fry feeders make a huge commotion, with fry bouncing everywhere in blind-eyed panic. And yet, I have found the reverse to be the case. Often fry feeding is subtlety itself, far more akin to dry fly or nymph feeding.

The other remarkable thing I have found is just how shallow the water is where this type of feeding takes place – mere inches rather than feet – so the angler has even more reason to tread cautiously, dress sombrely, and cast more carefully than usual. It is also about walking and looking – don't stay put! The fish won't and neither should you, unless, of course, you are in an area particularly known for this type of activity.

THE PATTERNS

Whatever I use, I make sure that I match the size – be this half an inch or four inches. Trout, when feeding on fry, can be very selective of size. Minkies, such as Dan's Fry (shown) and FM Suspender Minky, and Crystal River deer-hair fry patterns are all great. I do, though, tend to tie my Flat Roach on a curved hook (shown) to mimic the stunned, curved mannerism of the actual fry.

I also carry some traditionals. These are used on the dropper or occasionally when the trout switch their attention to very small fish. A Silver Invicta is still a marvellous fry pattern, and don't forget classics such as the fry design favoured by Arthur Cove – Wickham's Fancy. You could also put Appetisers, Missionaries and so on in that list, but limit your number of patterns. Everything I need for a day's fishing (even a small thermos) can be easily accommodated in a waistcoat – this ensures mobility at all times.

CLUES

It is important to gather all the information that you can. Gulls, terns (if they are still resident), small fish scattering and trout rising, of course – anything that looks out of place may lead you to where trout are prowling. Be alert to all these, and other, possibilities; follow hunches, too.

THE APPROACH

If the trout are working a shoreline (and in very shallow water) it makes perfect sense to keep a low profile and not spook them. By kneeling away from the water (position B), and also casting along the shore (position A) – especially if you can break up your silhouette by standing amid weed – you will remain largely unseen by the fish and improve your chances in thin water. Actually, how you fish is often more important than what you fish, so keep low!

Needless to say, this is a floating-line operation with a leader able to turn over the chosen pattern, and also give a degree of presentation. I would, therefore, urge a long leader of 14 feet or more and a sufficiently strong tippet to hold the size of fly you intend using.

Good hunting.

Life's A *Beach*

Arguably the trickiest to catch, the mullet is the hardest fighting of our coastal species… but it isn't an impossible target, says Austen Goldsmith.

Name: Austen Goldsmith
Lives: Porthleven, Cornwall
Occupation: Saltwater fly fishing guide and owner of uksaltwaterflies.com
Fishing saltwater for: 10 years
Favourite venue: The Lizard Peninsula, Cornwall
Contact: www.uksaltwaterflies.com

FIRST ENCOUNTERS

My first encounter was in Ireland, where we fished breadflake using light float tackle on 4lb line and old centrepin reels. I had a memorable morning, sight fishing for mullet in shallow water and landing fish to about 5lb.

I now had the bug and returned to the same location a few days later, determined to capture one with the fly rod. After a short while, I landed a mullet using a white-chenille fly, fished static under an indicator and over bread for groundbait.

Despite the success, it felt like cheating. By all means fish bread tactics and have some fun but try using your head and not your 'loaf'. We are fly fishermen and we match the hatch!

Get in! Mullet are often hard to catch, so when you get one, the satisfaction is incredible!

MATCHING THE HATCH

The following July found me in Ireland again, and while bass fishing I witnessed a large hatch of sand hoppers. These crustaceans congregate in the weed piled up on some beaches that begins to rot in the same manner as a compost heap. The next spring tides see the hoppers washed into the sea. Both the mullet and the seagulls know when it's time to feed and you often see them feasting alongside one another.

The sand hopper is one of the mullet's favourite snacks (illustration courtesy of Kendall Bio Research).

It is worth remembering that the same circumstances can also result in a hatch of seaweed maggots. The mullet and bass will feed on them with the same gusto as the hoppers, so always take along a few simple, white bugs. The bass fishing had been so good that first morning that I had virtually ignored the mullet shoal feeding in the surface film 10 yards out.

The following morning the bass had vanished but the mullet were still there and feeding. My attention was drawn towards them and I had three good-sized mullet to about 4lb on trout flies – all hooked virtually under the rod tip.

Later in the autumn the same sequence of events took place at home in Cornwall. I had been fishing a local beach for a few days as the spring tides grew to an all-year high. I had taken a few good bass including a seven-pounder and an eight-pounder.

When sand hoppers are washed into the sea, mullet and seagulls will feed avidly.

As the tides grew, so did the number of sand hoppers scurrying away from the breaking waves. Once again a large shoal of mullet were feeding within a few yards of the shore and I hooked and lost a couple of bruisers.

These fish had one intention… and that was to head out to sea at great speed!

THE FISH

There are three types of mullet inhabiting home waters. Thin-lipped mullet grow to between 2lb and 3lb and a large one would be 5lb. Number two is the golden grey mullet, the smallest of the mullet with a 2lb fish being a specimen. The third type, and the one featured in this article, is the thick-lipped mullet. This is the fish you will encounter on a regular basis and which can grow to double figures.

They live on a diet of small invertebrates, fine particles and microscopic algae. It is worth remembering that mullet, like bass, have very slow growth rates, and a 5lb mullet could well be 20 years old. So please practice catch and release at all times.

(Ed: I've yet to taste one that's tasted any good!)

WHAT TO LOOK FOR

Look for areas where seaweed is piled up, steep beaches and boulder-strewn corners. A storm during spring tides will allow the sea weed to pile up higher than produce the average tide line and, given a couple of weeks of mild weather, will start to ferment.

Flies may lay their eggs in the weed, or sand hoppers may take residence providing the weed is not dislodged by further storms or tides. When the next big tides start to hit the weed, the hoppers and maggots will be washed into the sea.

The trick is to get to know a few spots and try to keep an eye on them during the weeks prior to a potential hatch. Revisit sites and give the weed a good turning over and look for signs of life.

Sand smelt may also appear and begin to feed alongside the mullet. These look like miniature tarpon at around four inches long. Bass may well be around, feeding on sand smelt and the hatching maggots and hoppers. So a few casts with a baitfish pattern are always worth trying in the area.

WHEN TO FISH

You could encounter a hatch between June and October. During the three days prior to and during a big spring tide, mullet seem to arrive two hours before high tide and leave two hours after.

Methods

A Pheasant Tail Nymph seems to do the business when it comes to mullet fishing.

RODS

You can fish with any 6/7-wt fly rod because you will rarely need to cast out more than 15 yards. Saltwater fittings are obviously preferable, although trout rods will do – just be sure to rinse all the fittings afterwards

REELS

You definitely want quality reels that will take a decent amount of backing. Mullet can run a long way, very quickly!

LINES

Floating lines are perfect in this situation.

LEADER SETUP

You will generally be fishing in dirty water during a hatch. This is a bonus because mullet are very line shy in clear water. I fish with a 6ft, 10 lb

and tackle

After a hectic battle, a mullet finally tires close to the kelp.

copolymer leader. The reason for the short leader is that there is generally a lot of debris floating on the surface. The longer the leader is, the more likely it is to get snagged up and broken. However, if you are spooking fish then try a longer leader.

A strike indicator will help to keep the flies in the feeding zone and will detect bites. A gang of three flies will also increase your chances of a hook-up; you have to remember that there is a lot of food in the water, so the more flies you present, the better your chances. Keep the droppers short because mullet will be filter feeding in the surface and just below it.

FLIES

Sand hoppers are nocturnal creatures that will burrow and hide in gravel or rotting weed. So far, I have found Pheasant Tail Nymphs to be an excellent match for hoppers, although I have no doubt that grayling bugs will work too.

Don't be afraid to use some flashy materials in the dressing, as the water will be murky… gold ribbing will get the fish's attention. I have also developed a fly to go on the point of the leader. I call this the Team Leader.

Its purpose is to prevent the team of nymphs from sinking too deep, hence the foam body. Any wave motion and this will sink the team of flies, so you need to be constantly treating the leader with floatant before recasting.

LINE TRAY

You 'must' use a line tray; to fish without one in this situation would be a disaster. If the line touches the weed it will be buried in seconds.

It's there! A mullet on a fly is a challenge for even the most experienced angler.

The rotting weed in the foreground will hold vast swarms of sand hoppers; the flies below should do the trick!

TEAM LEADER (POINT FLY)
Hook: Partridge CS 54 saltwater shrimp, size 10
Thread: Dyneema **Body:** Bronze Loco Foam
Tail: Rainbow Krystal Flash or similar **Legs:** Pheasant tail feather
Rib: Gold wire

PHEASANT TAIL NYMPH (DROPPERS)
Hook: Partridge L2A, size 14 **Thread:** Dyneema
Body: Pheasant tail fibres **Rib:** Gold tinsel or wire
Thorax: Pheasant tail fibres **Thorax cover:** Pheasant tail fibres

Please trust me on this one – it can be a nightmare!

LANDING NET
This is absolutely essential, as you will not be able to beach any fish through the weed.

FISHING METHOD
It's all very simple stuff really. You wade out through smelly, rotting seaweed and you get knocked about by the shore break while standing on slippery rocks trying to keep the line in the line tray and clear of loose weed.

Your gang of flies will constantly sink and get debris attached, so you just put up with this and recast. You may have 50 to 100 fish within a few yards of your rod tip and this can be frustrating, so just bite your lip and hold your breath as the feeding shoal zigzags past your fly over and over again.

You may struggle to distinguish a take in the surging water, so just keep striking at any suspicious movement of the controller. Eventually, your leader or controller will slide away from you and you will get a hook-up. That's when the fun starts and

the line begins whizzing back out through the rings.

As I have mentioned before, saltwater fly fishing requires leg work, research and time. Providing you have put in the time, kept your eyes open and studied the tide tables, you will succeed.

So, before you head off to the shoreline, be sure to pack a couple of indicators and a few trout flies in the standard saltwater flies. There are other ways of catching mullet on the fly and I hope to cover this issue in future articles.

Good luck, AG.

CATCH MORE EVERY MONTH...

Grab your favourite fishing reads on the go!

Available in single issues or save £££s with a variety of subscription offers – see in app for details.

Also available for BlackBerry, PC and Mac at pocketmags.com

To get the required app, simply search for the magazine title in your app store or at pocketmags.com

Tide *tigers!*

Cornish guide Graham Bray takes to the south coast and explains the trials and tribulations of tackling bass. It's not for the faint-hearted, but damn, it's as wild as it gets.

*t*hanks to the banning of pair trawling within six miles of the coastline and the recognition that stocks wouldn't last perhaps as long as once thought, the bass is making a revival.

Bass inhabit many different features of the British coast. Fish in their early years can be reliably found in large schools, following the tide up most estuaries of the southern half of the UK. Deep-water reefs offshore act as magnets to the boat anglers, who regularly come into contact with the bigger boys while fishing with live, large sandeels or, more commonly, live whole mackerel. The vast expanses of West Country Atlantic storm beaches, where anglers 'cast at the third breaker' using 12ft and 13ft beachcasters and multipliers, are long-established favourites. The rock-hopper too is a unique species, clambering down cliff faces and fishing neat parcels of peeler crab, in tiny gullies, using souped-up carp kit for the big, solitary bruisers of the bass world. They are, in essence, our premier game fish in the sea and have, in the last 10 years, taken the fly fishing world by storm.

One of the prime targets for the specimen-hunting bass fisher is the rocky coast. You only have to check out a rock pool at low tide to see the myriad of creatures that this landscape holds and this rich feeding opportunity acts as a magnet for this aggressive fish.

SO WHAT MAKES A GOOD BASS MARK?

*t*his is a simple recipe really.

Take a bay, perhaps somewhere off the coasts of Devon, Cornwall, Wales or Southern Ireland, among others.

It would ideally regularly endure a bit of a battering from an onshore swell - white water is good water.

Add lots of rocks (the more the better).

Dividing these rocks should be gullies, potholes, ridges and lots of other nice features that become visible at low tide.

Inside these gullies, alongside the rocks, and on the sea bed, there should almost always be kelp. This acts as shelter for the bass' prey.

The mark should also allow you to make casts into the breakers – a veritable washing machine of bass food – in relative safety.

The less fished your chosen mark is, the better. Bass anglers are the most secretive of all!

One of my favourite tricks is to pick a very calm day (safety first) and go for a swim. It's not unusual for me to walk and swim three or four miles of coastline in search of a new mark to try.

Even a small swell will improve your chances of catching from the rocks.

Sharp bits galore. Take a towel with you and wet it before handling bass.

SAFETY ADVICE AND RULES

ur coastguards have enough of their time wasted by dopey beachgoers that insist on taking inflatables to sea with them. Therefore: If you cannot swim or don't enjoy getting wet, this is not for you.

I would also only advise this type of fishing for those that are physically fit.

Beware of being cut off – know the tide times. You MUST have a clear entrance and escape route.

Always, always, always tell someone when and where you are going.

Bear in mind that mobile phone reception is often pretty scarce on the coast.

Wear sun block and a hat, even on overcast days, and take a bottle of water.

Take a cloth to use when handling bass – their dorsal fins and gill plates are very sharp indeed.

Do not take large tackle bags and heavy, tackle-laden waistcoats.

There is a legal minimum-size limit of 40cm for bass.

Many estuaries are now official nursery areas and, as such, have various rules and regulations that must be adhered to.

he mark featured in these pictures is a favourite of mine in St Austell Bay, off the south coast of Cornwall. This mark illustrates perfectly the sort of ground you should look for. It's a bit of a hike down the cliffs, which is good – few others will know it's there, let alone bother to make it – and has plenty of ridges of rock and deep gullies.

A brisk onshore wind will stir up a good swell and I've found that the best sessions of all are what the Newquay surf bums would term 'gnarly'. Yep, when there's four feet of white water rolling onto those gullies, get out there. I'm not sure quite why the bass love the surf so much. It must be the amount of dislodged, tumbling food present, coupled with the cover of cloudy water.

This particular mark features long ridges of kelp-covered rock running parallel to the beach. The bass use the channels between the ridges as 'feeding lanes' and, therefore, this is where you need to get your fly.

The trick is to cast behind the crest of the wave, just as it breaks. By using a sinking shooting head, the line cuts into the rear of the wave and drops into the gulley. The bigger the waves, the faster sinking the line I'll use – you need to get it down and out of the grasp of the white water.

As soon as it reaches fishing depth I've found that erratic, long strips – almost as fast as you can go – do the damage. When you feel that fish, hit it. Hard. Bass have tough mouths and you do need to set that hook.

Please bear in mind that bass are a very slow-growing species and while they are one of the finest eating fish in the UK, you should limit your kill. Taking the odd fish is of course a great reward for your hard work, but make sure it is only the odd fish!

KIT LIST

Rod: 9-10ft 8/10-wt
Reel: Saltwaterproof or anything you don't mind wrecking. A good drag is handy, but not essential – bass are tough but they're not tarpon. Wash it after use.
Line: Something cheap – rocks and fly lines don't get on. I use bargain shooting heads in intermediate and medium to fast sinking.
Leader: 14lb to 20lb. This is more to help against abrasion from rocks. I use Toothy Critter tapered jobs to help turn over large flies, but it's not essential.
Line tray: You need one of these. It stops your line getting properly mangled by the rocks and surf. Pick one that'll take a battering.
Footwear: Old trainers or flip-flops. Wear something that will grip on the rocks and that you don't mind getting wet. Wearing wellies or (especially) waders is downright dangerous.

The coastguards have their work cut out in the summer – don't make more work for them!

IMPROVE YOUR CATCH RATE

Here are some tips to boost your catches. Please bear in mind that these may not ring true in all situations or locations, but for late summer and autumn bassing off the south coast of Devon and Cornwall, they'll work!

Tides: Buy a tide table (about 50p) and study it. I've found that neap (the opposite to spring) tides are best. I usually aim to make the first cast at around one hour before the bottom of the tide.

Swell: I've found that three to four feet of choppy breakers is the best. Any less and the fish don't seem to take as confidently, any more and it gets a bit hazardous.

Flies: Use small ones (size 4 to 2) when it's calm and clear, and bigger ones (size 1 to 3/0) when the surf gets up. My top fly is a Black and Silver Eel in a size 1.

Casting: Learn to haul. This is a big bonus, because when the swell's up it tends to be windy. You must learn to cast a large fly on a heavy line, sometimes a long way.

Playing Fish: Bass can be crafty buggers. They'll often head straight for the crest of the wave – as if surfing – and use the full force against you. I lost what would have been my best fish because of this.

Fish Every Inch: Spend time on obvious hotspots, but also keep moving to cover every pit, gulley and ridge. The more water you cover, the more chance you have. Bass will chase sandeels, crabs and shrimps in less than a foot of water – remember this!

BLACK AND SILVER EEL (A TOP ALL-ROUNDER!)

Hook: Saltwater long-shank size 6 to 1/0 **Body:** Flat gold tinsel
Tail: Pearl and silver Crinkleflash or Krystal Flash **Wing(1):** Pearl and silver Crinkleflash or Krystal Flash **Wing(2):** Black Crinkleflash or Krystal Flash
Head: Black thread with eyes painted on. Cover first two-thirds of hook shank and dressing with epoxy resin

Presenting nymphs at range can be tricky, but with the help of a guide, anglers can soon get the hang of it.

A Guide To
guiding

Andrew Ryan has been a fly fishing guide since he was a teenager. Here he explains the rudiments needed for anyone wishing to follow in his footsteps.

i have been a guide – mainly on my local water, which just happens to be Ireland's world-famous River Suir – for more than 20 years. I started at the tender age of 16 before gaining a string of qualifications in my chosen career. And I can honestly say that guiding has helped me meet some of the most amazing and interesting people on the planet, from mega-wealthy CEOs of international companies to the normal blokes in the street.

My guiding experience has mainly been in Ireland, but in my twenties I also worked for a guiding operation in Argentina in northern Patagonia, close to the town of Esquel. The description of 'fishing guide' may conjure up images of someone being paid to spend hours on the riverbank or lakeside catching loads of fish, but the truth is that a good guide NEVER fishes while standing alongside a client!

I've worked with a couple of American guides who hailed from Montana, and their style was a real eye-opener compared to what I was used to! They were hard-nosed, tobacco-chewing, take-no-crap kind of guys,

but really knew what they were doing. They took no nonsense from anyone – their clients, employer or other guides – but their objective was ALWAYS to ensure a good day's fishing for their clients. However rough around the edges they were, the care and attention they gave clients was impressive.

The pair now run a company called Patagonia River Guides, which is one of the most professionally run in Argentina.

The fishing isn't always great in Ireland and you have to take the good with the bad. What makes a guide stand out is his ability to turn poor conditions into a memorable day for the client. Irish rivers are very prone to bad flooding, so alternative methods and a little bit of coaching can turn an otherwise bad day for the client into a learning experience that will further their abilities in fly fishing. This can come in many forms, be it improving their fishing techniques or a little bit of casting tuition.

Often when the rivers are flooded I like to get out the heavy artillery and start fishing with streamer patterns. It

Andrew stretches to net a trout for American client Michael Pcolinski, who experiences first hand just how effective a good guide can be.

»

may horrify some anglers but it is an exceptional method for fishing swollen rivers and is one of my favourite styles, as it tends to attract the larger fish in the system. Just one or two of those big trout coming to the fly will change an angler's opinion on this style of fishing.

In my experience, clients can be very varied and will have different expectations from their day. I like to discover their needs and desires before we start, such as whether they want to catch loads of fish or learn new techniques.

Clients also come with different levels of experience – some are very competent, some are poor casters and just get by on the river, some are serious anglers wanting to hone their skills and some know more than you do! I usually break clients down into four categories – day-trippers, novices, know-it-alls and serious anglers.

DAY-TRIPPERS
The day-trippers are easiest to please. They usually want to have a great day out, a nice lunch, a few fish and just

generally say they went fishing in Ireland and have the photos to prove it. They are great fun, easy to please and just want to fish for one day at the time.

NOVICE ANGLERS
Some don't even realise they are novices but they are great fun because they are full of enthusiasm and eager to learn, sometimes wanting to pack too much into the day. From a guide's perspective they can be difficult to please as they often overestimate their

Nymphs are always a good bet for river fishing. They work even better suspended below a dry – it gives the client something to focus on!

Be sure to have plenty of flies, as you'll be guiding a lot of beginners and you can expect to lose plenty.

As a guide, you need to be able to keep your clients' spirits up throughout the day, a tough call when the fishing is hard. Andy keeps the guys smiling, though.

«

own abilities and expect to catch a lot. But with a little help this eagerness can be turned into passion, as they make for great anglers with serious dedication and a willingness to learn.

SERIOUS ANGLERS

These are pretty much the same as the aforementioned novices, but with a lot more experience and casting ability. Last year I had the pleasure of guiding a client from the USA, Phil Gay, who was a Master Caster and on the board of governors of the FFF (International Federation Of Fly Fishers). Phil is an amazing caster and one of the easiest people I have ever had to guide. I first met him in the States a few years ago when he tested me for my own Masters exam. Guiding a client that you can just point to where the fish are and he can get the fly there first time is amazing. I don't think I have guided anyone who caught as many trout so quickly as he did. He guides in the US and it is amazing how many of the tips and tricks are the same over there as here. One of my habits when guiding is to hold the client's fly, so he can't cast, and walk him up the river so as not to spook fish. I had never really noticed this, but Phil pointed out that he does exactly the same, and calls it 'walking the dog'.

KNOW-IT-ALLS

These are very common and the most difficult to guide. They usually have all the latest gear, loads of flies and have fished in all the best places. Their abilities may not be as good as they lead you to believe, but they are quick to point out that they don't really need a guide and just need you to show them where to go.

A couple of years ago I experienced the most frustrating morning of my career. The fishing conditions were perfect, the water was ideal, the weather was really warm… but no fish were being caught. Prospects looked poor and I suggested my client tie on one of my flies. His response was that he only fished with flies he tied himself. When I suggested he cast where I knew the trout were, he would cast in the opposite direction. When I advised short casts he would go long.

Before lunch I asked him if he understood my accent and he seemed a bit surprised as he replied he did. Then I said: "Well, why don't you do as you are being advised?" and informed him that I was returning to the shop and that he could fish on his own for the afternoon and there would be no charge.

He immediately apologised and explained that the last guide who

took him out had ripped him off. He changed tactics for the afternoon, starting using some of my flies and enjoyed a fantastic few hours. He was in fact a really good caster and an excellent angler. It turned out he was the CEO of a major US corporation and no-one had ever told him what to do. We have remained great friends ever since.

Many of the traits you need to be a guide are obvious and well documented. Health and safety, good knowledge of casting, local knowledge and etiquette are all very important, but what makes a guide stand out from the crowd is good customer service – being able to understand the requirements of a client, getting a feel for what they want from the day and ensuring that their expectations are not just fulfilled but exceeded. This is not always easy as conditions are often against us, so having a plan B and even a plan C is a necessity.

WHY USE A GUIDE?

With experienced clients you are being paid because of your local knowledge; they want to get onto the best spots without having to waste time. A guide's knowledge of the beats or river is paramount, not only knowing where the best spots are but also how to fish

ANDY RYAN ON GUIDING

I started guiding at the age of 16 – more than 20 years ago – after seeing guests from all over the world fishing the famous River Suir while staying at my parents B&B. I started to tag along with these visitors, learning some of the techniques they were using and adapting them to suit the local rivers. French and US anglers have had a huge influence on the way I fish, in particular the style of flies that French anglers use.

After accompanying these foreign anglers and helping them to catch more fish for a couple of years I decided to do my REFFIS (Register of Experienced Fly Fishing Instructors and Schools) Instructor exams in 1993, which meant I was also able to offer casting instruction as well as guiding. After this I joined STANIC (Salmon & Trout Association's National Instructors Certificate) in 1995, APGAI (Advanced Professional Game Angling Instructors) in 2001 before doing my FFF Masters and THCI (Two Handed Casting Instructors) in the USA. My personal feeling is that for a fishing guide to be most effective for the client some level of casting qualification is necessary. Very few clients are expert casters and need some help, tips and encouragement along the way.

There are now quite a few courses and paths to getting into guiding. In Ireland this year APGAI Ireland is launching a new guiding qualification and it is a great way of getting into a very worthwhile career. The course offers training in many aspects of guiding and also a one-year membership to APGAI Ireland, which includes your annual insurance.

those sections. For example, some sections will fish better with a dry fly, some will produce more with nymphs, and this is the kind of information a client is looking for.

It is not enough to lead them to the water and tell them that the fish are in there and leave them to their own devices. I like to initially talk them though the piece of water, explain why we will fish it a certain way, so that in future they will be more competent to fish with confidence on their own.

When the water's up and dirty don't give up – get the 'streamers' out! These flies will often save the day when fishing in coloured water.

DON'T EXPECT TO FISH

In recent years it has become fashionable to get into guiding as a career, but it takes a lot of hard work and dedication to really do your job correctly. For anyone wishing to become a guide, you will need to go and visit some of the top names in the profession and get some guiding from them first.

Often the perception is that guiding is about fishing all the time, and you will get to spend lots of time catching loads of trout. I never fish when guiding, I am at the client's shoulder all day, helping and instructing, ensuring they have a great day out. Now and again I have a cast in order to show and demonstrate, and this is a good way to help a client's confidence and to demonstrate that there are fish in there. However, far too often I hear tales of guides taking clients out, informing them of where the fish are then proceeding to fish themselves.

SAVE £££s ON THIS GREAT FLY FISHING MAGAZINE

ON SALE 2ND THURSDAY OF EVERY MONTH.

>> Total FlyFisher is aimed at fly anglers with an appetite for instruction.

Written by experts with a die-hard passion for the sport, their aim is to help you improve your skills and become a more effective angler in areas like casting and fly tying. It's informative, helpful, honest and trusted by thousands.

Featuring some of the UK's highest-profile contributors, great interviews, honest tackle reviews and dedicated venue and fly-tying sections, it's the read the modern fly angler shouldn't be without!

GET THE NEXT SIX ISSUES FOR JUST £16.74*

'Pop' On A Minkie!

Fishery manager Andy Miller reveals the secrets of tempting his Eyebrook trout to passionate fly fisherman and rock musician Colin Hodgkinson, during a late-season bank session.

he shoal of roach fry was well aware of the silver-flanked rainbow trout paying them more than a passing interest. But the ferocity and speed of the attack when it came took the small fish completely by surprise.

Scattering in all directions, the fry leapt clear of the lake's surface in an attempt to avoid the marauding trout fully intent on causing some serious damage. Stunned, limp victims lay helpless as the trout turned to survey the attack. Two, three, four and more fry were quickly swallowed and the

rainbow, more than pleased with its efforts, returned to its patrol of the lake's weed bed in search of more victims.

TELLTALE SIGNS

Strangely, this ferocity is not the only visible sign to look out for. Feeding trout can announce their presence as delicately as a light dimpled rise as they sip in the stunned fry. However, it is normally major water disturbance that's the dead giveaway. Then it's time to make your cast directly into the middle of the disturbance.

These swirls are very different to the normal trout rises you see, where it's important to establish the direction of the moving fish and cast a few feet in front. Here it's not! Attacking fish will turn quickly and return to the scene of their crime, so covering the initial disturbance is of prime importance.

EYEBROOK

Recognised as one of the country's most popular stillwater reservoirs, Eyebrook sits on the borders of three counties – Leicestershire, Rutland and Northamptonshire. It was built in 1940 by Stewart & Lloyds primarily to supply water to the nearby steelworks.

The reservoir was initially stocked with fingerling brown trout and opened its doors for fishing in 1952 as an any-method fishery. Over the decades the fishery has gone from strength to strength, converting to fly only, and now stocks rainbow trout to complement its head of resident brownies. Surrounded by rolling countryside, many famous stillwater game anglers, including Cyril Inwood, Arthur Cove, Gordon Fraser and Bob Carnhill, plied their trade here, developing some of their best-known patterns.

As an important habitat for wildlife, the reservoir was designated a Site of Special Scientific Interest in 1956.

WEATHER CONDITIONS

Andy Miller has been working here at Eyebrook for the best part of 20 years. Today rock musician Colin Hodgkinson, taking a break from his extensive touring programme, joins Andy on the banks of the water to target the fry-feeding trout.

"Over the past couple of days the trout have been moving close in across the top of the Island and along the bank down to Sam's Dyke. They seem to be taking both corixa and sticklebacks but not the roach and perch fry as yet," Andy explains. "Our weed growth has been pretty poor this year. In fact, the weed is so light that we had to cancel the annual weed-cutting operation, but we still have a few established beds, owing to the high levels of water in the reservoir. That high water hinders the light refraction that gets through to the weed and encourages it to grow.

"All along this area we're going to fish today there's a decent depth of water over a large weed bed and the trout are patrolling across the top and along the edges of it.

"Unfortunately we have a stiff westerly breeze blowing today that will cause me some casting problems, but it's not too bad for Colin as he's a left-hander. Nevertheless, it's not exactly what we needed. Ideally, it wants to be a lightish ripple, just enough to conceal the leader, but not so rough that you can't see the fish move. Sadly, today we have the latter, so it could be a bit of a struggle."

STOUT TACKLE

Andy tackles up a 10ft 7-wt rod, floating line and a single Popper Minkie on a 12ft leader. "I always use 10lb Maxima mono for my leader material; I like it to sit in the surface film, and not sink. Heavy fluorocarbon has a tendency to sink pretty quickly and that, in my opinion, will hinder my striking capability. Untreated mono sits on the surface film, or in it when de-greased with Fullers Earth, so I am totally in touch with my fly at all times. It can be a bit of a problem when conditions are flat calm but it's unlikely to be troublesome today."

Andy also has a view on mixing mono and fluorocarbon leader materials: "I can't see the problem. I often tie on a section of fluorocarbon to a mono butt when I'm fishing dry flies. It means that the leader, a couple of feet behind the fly, has a chance to sink slightly sub-surface without subjecting the dry fly to a complete soaking when it's retrieved. I know there's plenty of opinion that says

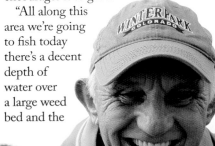

Andy helps Colin Hodgkinson out with his first proper fry feeder, taken on a Popper Minky in two feet of water.

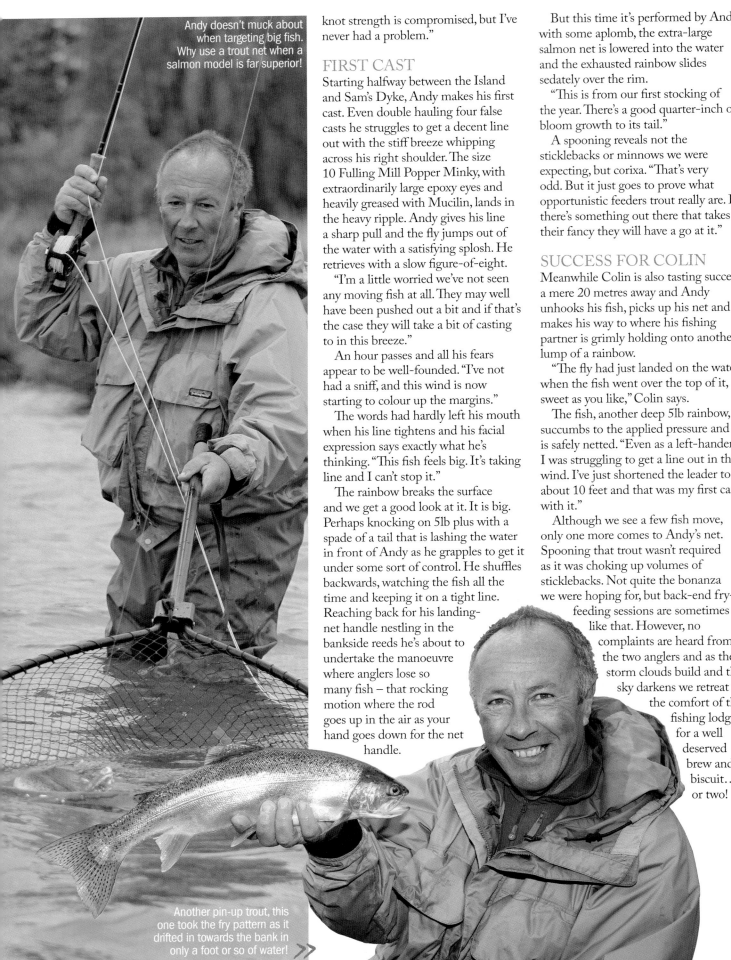

Andy doesn't muck about when targeting big fish. Why use a trout net when a salmon model is far superior!

knot strength is compromised, but I've never had a problem."

FIRST CAST

Starting halfway between the Island and Sam's Dyke, Andy makes his first cast. Even double hauling four false casts he struggles to get a decent line out with the stiff breeze whipping across his right shoulder. The size 10 Fulling Mill Popper Minky, with extraordinarily large epoxy eyes and heavily greased with Mucilin, lands in the heavy ripple. Andy gives his line a sharp pull and the fly jumps out of the water with a satisfying splosh. He retrieves with a slow figure-of-eight.

"I'm a little worried we've not seen any moving fish at all. They may well have been pushed out a bit and if that's the case they will take a bit of casting to in this breeze."

An hour passes and all his fears appear to be well-founded. "I've not had a sniff, and this wind is now starting to colour up the margins."

The words had hardly left his mouth when his line tightens and his facial expression says exactly what he's thinking. "This fish feels big. It's taking line and I can't stop it."

The rainbow breaks the surface and we get a good look at it. It is big. Perhaps knocking on 5lb plus with a spade of a tail that is lashing the water in front of Andy as he grapples to get it under some sort of control. He shuffles backwards, watching the fish all the time and keeping it on a tight line. Reaching back for his landing-net handle nestling in the bankside reeds he's about to undertake the manoeuvre where anglers lose so many fish – that rocking motion where the rod goes up in the air as your hand goes down for the net handle.

But this time it's performed by Andy with some aplomb, the extra-large salmon net is lowered into the water and the exhausted rainbow slides sedately over the rim.

"This is from our first stocking of the year. There's a good quarter-inch of bloom growth to its tail."

A spooning reveals not the sticklebacks or minnows we were expecting, but corixa. "That's very odd. But it just goes to prove what opportunistic feeders trout really are. If there's something out there that takes their fancy they will have a go at it."

SUCCESS FOR COLIN

Meanwhile Colin is also tasting success a mere 20 metres away and Andy unhooks his fish, picks up his net and makes his way to where his fishing partner is grimly holding onto another lump of a rainbow.

"The fly had just landed on the water when the fish went over the top of it, sweet as you like," Colin says.

The fish, another deep 5lb rainbow, succumbs to the applied pressure and is safely netted. "Even as a left-hander I was struggling to get a line out in this wind. I've just shortened the leader to about 10 feet and that was my first cast with it."

Although we see a few fish move, only one more comes to Andy's net. Spooning that trout wasn't required as it was choking up volumes of sticklebacks. Not quite the bonanza we were hoping for, but back-end fry-feeding sessions are sometimes like that. However, no complaints are heard from the two anglers and as the storm clouds build and the sky darkens we retreat to the comfort of the fishing lodge for a well deserved brew and a biscuit… or two!

Another pin-up trout, this one took the fry pattern as it drifted in towards the bank in only a foot or so of water!

the Bloodworm

We reveal the one fly that the winter stillwater angler simply dare not ignore – it's the trout's favourite, the Bloodworm!

The midge, chironomid or buzzer, call it what you will, is the most common food item for stillwater trout. It is one of the few insects that is in abundance on most lakes throughout the year and as such is one of the most commonly imitated bugs.

There are four parts to the midge life cycle: egg, larva, pupa and adult. With the exception of the egg (now where did I put that size 50 hook?), all of the stages are worth imitating by the nymph and dry-fly angler.

The larval form of the midge, the bloodworm, lives among the debris – silt for example – on the lake bed or swims freely near the bottom. With a rich, red colour thanks to

the haemoglobin in its body fluids, this little wriggler is at the top of the trout's menu in cold weather. Although they are present throughout the year, the scarcity of other natural insects in the winter means that bloodworm can become the number one prey for trout.

Soon enough, the bloodworm gradually turns into the pupal form, hanging about in the mid-layers of the lake. That is, until a warmer day when the pupa ascends towards the lake's surface where it hatches into the adult insect before taking to the skies.

An understanding of this cycle gives us a strong hint as to how to fool trout. The bloodworm lives on the

bottom, the adult on the surface and the pupa somewhere in-between.

Bloodworm patterns are as easy or as difficult to tie as you want to make them. One of the favourites is simply a red-painted, curved hook. Others are so accurate that you'd need a magnifying glass to distinguish them from the real thing.

During the depths of winter, the water in lakes tends to be at its coolest and its clearest. This gives the educated trout greater opportunity to inspect your fly, so in this article we'll err on the side of caution and go for a half-clever one. Using Veniard's Magic Glass body material, creating perfect bloodworms is a cinch.

FISHING TIPS

Going back to the midge life cycle, we see that, as a bottom-dwelling bug, the bloodworm scores with the trout best when it is fished deep. While it can be fished as a single fly on a long leader, it's when it is in a team that it comes into its own.

In a team of three flies, put the bloodworm on the point and pupa imitations (some people call them buzzers) on the top two droppers. It helps if you know the approximate depth of water that you're fishing in, enabling you to match the depth with the length of leader. You should be aiming to fish the bloodworm in the bottom couple of feet of water.

When fishing from a boat, the technical bods among you may want to 'plumb' the water using a long piece of cord with a lead weight attached. Drop the weight over the side, pay out the cord until you hit bottom and then measure the length as you pull it back in.

While it's not everyone's cup of tea, by far the most effective and accurate way of correctly positioning your flies and holding them at the right depth is by using an indicator. You may want to use a buoyant fly on the top dropper for this, or using one of the many commercially available models; it doesn't really matter either way. For more details, see Masterminds in this issue.

The bloodworm, and its older brothers and sisters (the pupae), are little beasts that don't move in a hurry. Therefore, the most accurate way to imitate them is by not retrieving at all. Any ripple on the water's surface does the job for you, moving the flies in a natural manner. It can help to give the set-up a sharp twitch every now and again, attracting a cruising fish's attention; but more often than not, just leave it.

When sport is slow it has to be said that this is a pretty mind-numbing form of fishing, but when the fish are on, you'll slay 'em!

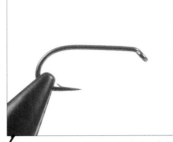

7 Mount the hook securely in the vice, leaving as much of the bend exposed as possible.

6 Wind the Magic Glass, keeping it firmly stretched, with the concave side uppermost. Stop when you get halfway up the shank.

VARIATIONS

Hot Head

Hook: Curved buzzer, sizes 8 to 14
Tail: Pearl Krystal Flash
Body: Red floss **Rib:** Red Flexi-floss
Head: Firefly Hot Head bead, red

Bloodworm

Hook: Curved buzzer, sizes 8 to 14
Tail: Red Body Stretch
Body: Red Body Stretch

3D Glass Bloodworm

Hook: Curved buzzer, sizes 8 to 14
Body: Red floss **Rib:** Fine pearl tinsel
Cheeks: Red holographic tinsel **Breathers:** White multi-yarn **Note:** Cover the whole of the body with epoxy resin

Flies supplied
by Fulling Mill

TYING THE MAGIC
Bloodworm

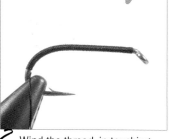

2 Wind the thread, in touching turns, from the eye of the hook to just around the bend.

3 Tie in a small, short pinch of red marabou from the base of the feather and trim the excess.

4 Take a length of Magic Glass and stretch it between your fingers a few times. This should warm it

5 Cutting the end to a point for neatness, tie in the Magic Glass, by the very tip, at the base of the

7 Tie off the Magic Glass, without trimming the excess, before dubbing the thread with a small pinch of seal's fur.

8 Wind the seal's fur up to the eye of the hook, keeping it relatively 'spikey'.

9 In open turns, wind the remaining Magic Glass over the seal's fur so that fibres stick out between the segments.

10 Tie off the Magic Glass and trim the excess. The seal's fur fibres can be clipped short if required.

11 Using tight turns with the thread, form a neat head and whip finish, or use three half-hitches.

12 Using a dubbing needle, apply a couple of drops of varnish to the head of the fly.

Strike It *lucky!*

Do you need some inspiration for the start of the season? Fear not! Charles Jardine is on hand to show you how to catch consistently in the cold.

*t*he perennial problem facing most early season anglers is just this – cold water! Irrespective of how cold the winter might have been, there is no getting away from the fact that from December, through March and certainly into April – possibly even May on our larger reservoirs like Grafham and Rutland – the water will be at its coolest. As anglers, we have to meet this challenge.

Of course, you could use the traditional early season combination, a winning one I should add, of a Hi-d/ Di7, short leader (we are talking 12 to 20 inches here) and buoyant flies: sort of working bottom-up approach. On the other hand, you might want to go top-down.

Either way, it is important to slow everything down. Your retrieve, your fly's movement and also the way the fly line moves. Why? Because the trout will have slowed down too! Cold water invariably closes down a trout's metabolic rate, in a similar way to us when experiencing cold; even given

the fact that while we can endure cold we are never truly at our most active. (Heat, of course, does the same thing and trout, like us, react in a similar way.) So, this month, here is a tactic to defy the coldest water and, conversely, the warmest too.

I give you, the static nymph!

TACTICS

Because we are talking cold water, the depth and location are key. But then, when aren't they?

In a majority of situations I would opt to use (if and where allowed), a multiple fly system. I think it offers far better depth options. Given the current crop of good indicators, by far the best available (and most prosaically titled), is the Fish Pimp series by Fulling Mill.

These can be cast extremely easily, hold a pattern at depth very well and, importantly, can be changed in an instant to alter that depth. So, even in successive casts a variety of water depths can be covered.

The next thing to concern us is the depth. If I know a water, especially during the early season, I will seek out shelves; places that have a defined apron of shallowish water descending quite abruptly to a much deeper area. Early season trout seem comfortable in these places and they feed confidently quite close to the bank.

Wherever possible, I also find areas close to the shore that I can fish along; meaning that you will need – and I at least crave for – banks with a minimum amount of angler pressure.

The next consideration is wind angle and velocity. Most will shun those banks with icy winds driving onto them. It makes sense; not only are they the coldest of places to fish and very unpleasant to stand in but, logically because of the wind driving the colder surface water towards you, are devoid of fish too.

Slow retrieves are the most effective.

But, quite oddly, I have found, especially on the smaller waters, that fish do seem to congregate in these areas. As long as you have depths greater than six feet – better, eight to 12 feet – and can get a cast out, you may well hit some seriously good fish.

Don't worry about trying to cast too far. I was fishing with Bill Rankin and we found all our fish a matter of 10 feet from the bank, in and around old reed beds. To make things even more interesting, the water was so cloudy that you imagined fish needing illuminated, high-intensity, low-light laser glasses in order to see anything.

One tactic I have used to some effect is to cast out a single, bead-headed pattern, one that is quite small on, say, a weighted, standard 10 hook. This setup is the only way I can get

Fishing close in on a downwind shore can be very successful – it's where the food is, after all.

THE INDICATED STATIC NYMPH

It is important, especially in deep bays to fish right around the margins

When the wind grips, and starts to swing the indicator and team of flies, you might need to mend line

Initial cast, allowing slack line to develop

Wind direction

If possible face the direction of the retrieve

Precision casting is needed to maximise catches during the winter months.

Allow slack to get the flies deeper in the water column

A tensioned line dragging the flies from the correct depth and fishing them too fast

a chartreuse, thoraxed Montana to work. This would be delivered with a good 10 to 12 feet of leader between the fly (a Montana, Gold Head, Daddy or Damsel) and the indicator. I would cast it out as far as I could into the wind and just let the surface wave action bring the whole thing back towards me, keeping in touch with the line leader and indicator with a hand-twist retrieve.

Let it keep coming right into the bank, or where the shelf or deep water gives out. Takes, though, are, or can be, subtlety itself. Often, given the wave movement, they will remain undetected but watch out for any sideways movement or curious diversions counter to the normal drift of the indicator. To these, and any other movements that look odd, just strike! You have nothing to lose… and everything to gain.

This is all very well if you have deep water. But what if you have to fish along a margin or indeed into a bay where you know, just know, there are fish? One, if not the, deadliest method of fishing an indicator is 'on the curve'.

Showing how undertow
will 'activate' static
fished patterns

PATTERNS

Actually, you can fish just about any pattern you like
but there are some that suit the style rather better
than others.

For digging in the depths and being almost a point
anchor, I would use:

A heavy, superglued Black Buzzer on size 6 to 10
grub hooks, or...

Carp Hook Buzzers, maybe Red Hook/Bloodworm
patterns on, again, heavy-wired, curved hooks.

If a smaller fly is required, try simple Black Buzzers
with a pearly rib with a silver (for murkyish water) or
black or copper (for really clear water), dressed on
size 10 to 16 hooks. A similar red-and-olive version
might be good.

For the dropper, almost any buzzer design, even
Crunchers and Diawl Bach, work extremely well.

For the top dropper, I rarely tend to look beyond a
Hare's Ear with or without a jungle cock cheek, tied
short on grub hooks in sizes 8 to 12. A quill buzzer
is another very good option and if the fish are being
very fussy, try a small (14 to 16), black, soft hackle.

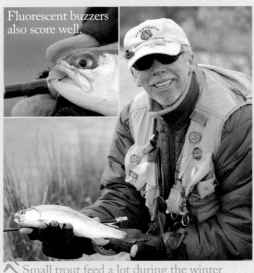

Fluorescent buzzers
also score well.

∧ Small trout feed a lot during the winter
months to remain healthy.

Quite frankly, there are few things
more fun in fishing than casting out
a buzzer or team of buzzers with an
indicator and just letting them gently
be teased around by the breeze in a
seductive curve. Fishing in this way
will tend to angle the patterns in
a climbing path at about 20 to 30
degrees to the surface – just like real
buzzers.

Takes, when they come (and they
will), tend to be felt even before the
indicator zips away. It is classic buzzer
fishing. And, when employing this
style, you can use longer leaders than
normal, given the angle prescribed
by the curve and path of the line's
direction.

All this is fine as long as you note
the word 'breeze'. If this area holds
fish and if you have anything more
than a breeze allowing your patterns
to trundle around on their own, it will
be nigh on fishless. Well, not always,
but the patterns will skid through
pretty fast and will not be as effective.

Thus you will need to understand
about slowing the whole movement
down by 'reverse odging'. This involves
walking down the bank almost in
time with the drifting indicator and
patterns, as opposed to walking a
curve into the patterns upwind which
is the classic Midlands' odging style.

There can be few more effective
early season styles than this, just so
long as the banks are clear of both
people and shrubs and you stay alert.
Again, takes can be very subtle.

In smaller bays and smaller water,
you can always 'throw' a mend into the

line to slow down the movement and
natural drift, as I have shown in the
diagram.

This aspect is hugely overlooked on
stillwaters… but do throw a slack-line
mend and not mend the tensioned

∧ Strikes need to be quick, you will
often feel the line move before the
indicator goes under!

line near to the indicator, which will only drag your patterns from their original position.

If you do find yourself fishing in that rare, early season 'creature', a flat calm, you can still enjoy the benefits of an indicated fly – and one, or three, often deeply sunk. But you will have to be a little more animated; more cunning. So, rather than casting out and using the wind, you will find it a great deal better to cast and allow the pattern(s) to settle. Then, after reaching their optimum depth, give a long, slow draw on the line to animate the flies upwards. Allow them to drift back down again and repeat it until the cast is fished out. On its day this method can be devastating.

By opting for one of these methods or, indeed, variations on the theme, just about any early season stillwater situation can be accommodated. Most importantly, you can still fish at depths that are the normal preserve of the sunken-line specialist, so combining not only the pleasure that a dry line gives with the joy and convenience of carrying just one line type.

Before closing on the early season, colder-water tactics, I would add a word to deflect some criticism levelled at this style of fishing. Fly fishing in this way is invariably subtle, requiring consummate understanding of the sub-surface topography, fish movement and also observation and concentration at the surface. Importantly, the angler is slowing the pattern and moving the whole affair in a very realistic manner.

Maybe, just maybe, it is a touch more skilful than many give it credit for, there is more to it than meets the eye. It is not legering, nor should it be so. Instead, wherever possible, it should mirror nature in the cold and the early season.

IN CONCLUSION

Now, all this may not be high art – but it is a far cry from the heinous crime against fly fishing that so many seem to portray the indicated static nymph as being. As I have pointed out, it is but another tactic at our disposal – not the Holy Grail! But, in cold water and when life is slow and takes are gentle, there are few better ways of presenting a fly or deceiving the cold-water 'wolves' that trout so often are at the season's earliest doors.

Takes next to the bank can come as a surprise if you are not awake!

Desert Island *flies*

Bob Barden, competition angler and head warden at Bewl, is the man who brought us anorexic nymphs. This month he shows us the three flies he couldn't live without…

KILLER

The first fly in my top three would be my very own 'Killer', so called because I couldn't think of anything else to call the thing.

This was always the first fly I attached to my leader. It didn't matter where or when I was fishing, even in competitions – on it went.

The most memorable time I had fishing this pattern was during my first international. I was fishing on the Lake Of Menteith in Scotland, the year was 1995, and it was just like being back at Bewl. It was almost flat calm with a hint of a ripple getting up. I managed to come seventh individually and third in the England team. Nearly half my bag was taken on this unassuming little fly.

Hook: Drennan traditional wet, size 8 **Thread: Green Body:** Sooty-olive seal's fur **Rib:** Copper wire **Tail:** Two medium or light-olive cock hackle tips

HARE'S EAR NYMPH

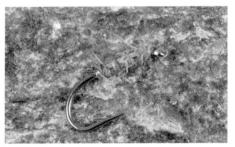

The Hare's Ear Nymph catches fish on all waters – still and running. It is especially effective on stillwaters where you get a good hatch of small green midge.

It can be tied with a pearl Mylar rib as shown, a silver rib or even with none at all.

Again, this fly has been a top competition pattern for me. Funnily enough, it seems to do best in calm conditions. A lot of people think that the fly won't get noticed but I actually think that the small, thin profile is more natural than some of the more bulky patterns that seem to be the norm – this is why it's so effective.

Hook: Kamasan B175 or Fulling Mill competition heavyweight, size 12 **Thread: Green Body:** Hare's ear fur **Rib:** Pearl Mylar

BUZZER

On opening day on Bewl, this, along with my Killer, will be the first fly on my leader – the Killer on the point and the Buzzer on the dropper. I'll be there, standing on the bank, drifting them around on the breeze – luvvly jubbly! They rarely let me down.

I've played about with body colour and the colour of the breathers and it appears that green and black are by far the best, along with the wool mentioned.

A friend of mine had a go with these patterns, playing about with the tyings, and one that he found very effective on rising trout was the green-bodied midge but tied with CDC, shuttlecock-style.

Hook: Kamasan B175, size 12 **Thread:** Black or green **Body:** Tying thread **Rib:** Silver wire **Breathers:** White, orange or peach wool

River & Stream

FEATURE FILM
SCAN FOR

#4/5

Introducing the lightest fly reels in the world*...

These lightweight river fishing reels are a marvel of modern day engineering and the envy of many. Both reels feature our new, innovative, adjusta-clicker drag system as we bring to the bank a product that truly challenges the boundaries of production technology with the reels weighing in at a staggering 50g (#2/3) and 58g (#4/5)...

*Lightest Aluminium CNC machine cut clicker-drag fly reels on the global market at time of launch: February 2013

PRODUCT VIDEO
SCAN FOR

Lightweight Fly Rods

Premium Luggage

RRP £139.99

Request our new catalogue at www.wychwood-tackle.co.uk

designed in Redditch, England by

Wychwood™

Czech *Mate!*

Do you want to catch a big winter grayling? Simon Robinson reveals his top methods to set you on the road towards a 3lb-plus lady of the stream.

Over recent years, Czech nymphing has become one of the most popular ways of catching grayling during the winter. The method is an excellent way of catching fish in even the coldest of conditions. It is also the perfect means of targeting big grayling, as I will explain later.

Czech nymphing was first brought back to this country by anglers visiting the Continent to take part in European and World Team events. The original pioneers of the tactic were the Czechs and Poles. It is now used all over the world as a very popular tactic if fish can't be seen moving on the surface. It is also commonly referred to as 'bugging'. In this article I will take you through the basics of the technique that has served me well for many seasons now.

THE BASICS

The technique of Czech nymphing involves the angler fishing a team of weighted nymphs on a short, fixed line. The angler rolls the flies upstream and tracks them with the rod tip as they drift past the angler's feet.

At the end of the cast, the flies rise and swing in the water. The angler can expect takes at any point during each cast, from the moment the nymphs hit the water to the final lift and swing at the end of the drift.

To put these tactics to the test I visited the Teviot in the Scottish Borders. This river is famous for its big grayling and on the day this proved to be the case again. The river produced several big, bottom-feeding grayling between two and two and a half pounds. However, the highlight of the

day was the 3lb-plus grayling that put up a tremendous fight and showed the quality of the fish that you can expect from this unique river. But how do you go about targeting these bigger grayling?

Although grayling do feed on the surface and can be taken on dry flies and surface spiders, they spend the vast majority of their time, particularly during the winter, feeding on or near the stream's bed. I have found over the years that the biggest grayling feed almost exclusively near the stream's bed.

So, if you want big grayling, I strongly suggest that you fish nymphs near the bottom. The main food items on the riverbed during winter are shrimps and caddis larvae, so, as you have probably guessed, it is not a bad idea to base your choice of Czech nymphs around these naturals.

The correct leader breaking strain will make the difference between catching fish and blanking.

THE TACKLE

I use a 10ft 6-wt Diamondback rod. I use a long rod, as this allows me to hold more line off the water. As a result, I get more control over the drift of my nymphs.

If you are trying this method for the first time don't be too worried about needing a specialist rod; your stillwater rod will cope adequately.

Which line? I use a 'special' line that I have developed purely for this technique. It is a Cortland 333 Zebra Strike indicator line. I like this because it is made up of alternate black and white sections. To the end of this line I attach a bright, braided loop. I use this bright orange loop as a visible indicator to register takes. The final white section of the line is then marked with a permanent marker to help register takes further up the line. It also helps to control the depth of the nymphs if the tip of the fly line is taken under the surface by the current or by very heavy nymphs.

Leaders should be made of heavy copolymer or fluorocarbon.

Heavy flies will catch on the bottom and fine line will mean that you will be forever tying up new leaders. Before selecting my leader, I first look at the clarity of the water.

If the water is very clear, I will opt for a copolymer

FASTER-WATER SET-UP

Marked Zebra line held vertically off water

Orange loop

10ft to 12ft

Current

18in to 22in between flies

SLOWER-WATER SET-UP

Watch orange loop for takes

Marked Zebra line

10ft to 12ft

Current

18in to 22in between flies

TWO-FLY CLEAR-WATER RIG

Marked Zebra line

Orange loop

10ft to 12ft

Current

3ft between flies

TOP TIP

Fish back down a pool if you have caught fish on the way up; you will often pick up more fish.

For fishing satisfaction, a large male grayling like this one is hard to beat.

Grayling can be caught right under your feet; walk slowly and fish thoroughly. »

The extra markings at the end of the line are to aid bite detection.

of around 5lb breaking strain. If, however, the water is particularly fast or coloured, I will go for a 6lb or 7lb fluorocarbon leader. Leader length should not be too long.

Remember that we are looking to fish at close range with control. I usually opt for a leader of around 10 to 12 feet, carrying either one or, more usually, two droppers. Flies need to be much closer together than for other forms of nymphing and I place my flies 18 to 22 inches apart.

SPOTTING TAKES

As described previously, takes can come at any point during the drift. The hard part is recognising them and hitting them quickly enough to make sure the grayling is well hooked. To do this, the angler must watch like a hawk for takes.

Takes are registered as any movement of the fly line or leader as the cast is tracked downstream. The takes vary enormously; most are seen as the fly line simply stopping dead during the drift. They can, however, be very subtle and on many occasions are a tiny pause or stab on the leader or fly line.

TOP TIP
Have a visible loop and marked fly line to register takes.

Takes can also be very positive and can be a definite pull on the fly line that can be felt at the hand. This is particularly true in areas of fast water, as the grayling have little time to inspect the angler's patterns.

In fast water, the angler is also tracking a much faster drift and the greater momentum makes the takes easier to feel. However, I would not recommend that you rely entirely on feel, as you will probably miss more takes than you register. As a general rule of thumb, I probably feel one in every five takes in fairly quick-moving water and in slower stretches I rarely feel any!

In every case you must strike immediately at any indication of a take. Grayling are masters of taking and ejecting possible food items very quickly. As anyone who has sight fished and watched them in clear water will tell you, you need to be alert.

WHERE TO FISH CZECH STYLE

During winter, grayling can be found anywhere on the river, from shallow riffles to deep, slow pools. However, there will always be areas where they are more likely to be found. In my experience, the best areas to Czech style for winter grayling are steady runs and pools of around three to five feet in depth. Look for areas with a nice steady flow, I have rarely found a lot of winter grayling in rapids or very turbulent water.

Look for areas where grayling can get out of the main current, either side of a boulder or in depressions in the riverbed are classic examples. Weed

beds are also good areas, as they hold a lot of food items, particularly shrimp.

THE METHOD

If I am fishing this style I will work my way through a pool systematically, with the aim of covering every inch of it. There is some debate about whether it is best to work up or down a pool.

I fish both ways, depending on the water conditions. If the water is clear, I like to work up a run, as I believe that there is less chance of spooking the fish. If the water is coloured I prefer to work down a pool, as this allows the angler to wade with the current and gives more control over the deadly final lift and swing of the drift. Whatever way you choose, do not worry about getting close to the fish. Grayling are very tolerant of waders, far more than trout, and will take your nymphs very close to your feet. In fact, I think that the disturbance of the angler wading can often disturb food items and induce the fish to feed.

Shrimps, caddis, all sorts really, will be easily dislodged by an angler wading. Fish are not stupid and they are very

your flies. For this reason it is vital that you carry a good selection of different weights.

These weights can come from a variety of sources including lead wire, tungsten beads and pre-leaded hooks. The various weights are used to control the drift in different depths and speeds of water. Experimentation is the key, but the aim is to get the fly travelling on or near the bottom as naturally as possible.

As a general rule, the faster or more powerful the water, the heavier the patterns needed. As a guide, if you are not feeling your fly touching the bottom at some point during your drift, you are probably fishing patterns that are too light. For this reason, you also need to be prepared to lose a few patterns on the bottom; unfortunately, it comes with the job!

If you are finding that you are losing too many flies, try using lighter leader for your droppers. Place the heaviest fly in the middle; this should reduce the number that you lose when you are snagged up. Alternatively, try using the tiny silver leader rings that are available.

Try to get a system whereby you

can identify the different weights of patterns. This will enable you to pick the correct weight for the conditions. Also, think about the hooks that you use. Grayling are fantastic fish and should be returned alive to the water. For this reason I strongly recommend that you fish with barbless hooks.

I tie my nymphs on various types of hooks. I tie on hooks from lightweight right through to heavy-wired carp hooks and I have tied a lot of my heavy grayling bugs on Kamasan B775 barbless hooks. Whatever you choose they need to have a heavy wire to help get the fly deep, yet have to be excellent fish holders. This is an important fact, as grayling twist and turn when hooked and will often be lost if your hooks are not high quality.

When it comes to the patterns themselves, I do not believe that the fly pattern makes a lot of difference. I have included some of my top patterns here, but I would recommend that you try your own patterns based on some basic themes.

Colours can be very important. I have fished days in clear water when fish will look at nothing other than

quick to latch onto any 'free' food source. Don't overlook a pod of fish that could be right under your nose.

For this reason I will often fish up a pool and then work back down, especially if I have caught fish or know grayling to be present. The fish could have latched onto food I have dislodged.

When fishing this style, the most important factor in controlling the drift of your patterns is the weight of

GOLD HEAD CADDIS
Hook: Kamasan B775/B110, size 8 or 10
Body: Hare's ear **Thorax:** Cream dubbing
Legs: Stripped golden pheasant
Head: Gold bead, brass or tungsten

PINK SHRIMP
Hook: Kamasan B775/B110, size 10 or
12 **Underbody:** Lead wire **Body:** Mix of pink
SLF and Light Brite **Rib:** Pink wire **Back:**
Pink balloon/nymph skin

SKINNY CZECH NYMPH
Hook: Kamasan B775/B110, size 10
Underbody: Lead wires **Body:** Nymph skin
Back: Dark brown thin skin **Legs:** Partridge
fibres

HARE'S EAR CZECH
Hook: Kamasan B775/B110, size 8 or 10
Underbody: Lead wire **Body:** Hare's ear
Rib: Gold tinsel **Back:** Thin skin
Over-rib: Monofilament/coloured wire

TAGGED GOLD HEAD
Hook: Kamasan B775/B110, size 8 or 10
Body: Hare's ear **Rib:** Gold wire
Tail: Bright floss, vary colours to suit
Head: Gold bead, brass or tungsten

HOTSPOT CZECH
Hook: Kamasan B775/B110, size 8 or 10
Underbody: Lead wire **Body:** Hare's ear
Thorax: Bright seal's fur **Rib:** Gold tinsel
Back: Thin skin **Over-rib:** Monofilament/
coloured wire

drab imitative patterns. Yet, on other days, bright colours really get grayling in a taking mood.

For this reason, I recommend that you carry a selection of Hare's Ears and other drab patterns, some patterns incorporating coloured spots or tags and some very bright shrimp patterns. Experimentation on the day will tell you what the fish prefer.

Simon's massive 3lb grayling... you'll have to try this form of fishing!

A Gold Head is another interesting ingredient. On some days the fish love it, and on others even a single Gold Head on the cast can put the fish off completely. For this reason I will always start with a selection, usually including a Gold Head, a nymph with colour and a drab imitative pattern. Do not be afraid to fish with two or three similar patterns if the fish dictate it.

Water conditions are also important when making your initial fly choices. If the water is gin clear, it is probably a good idea to scale down to just two flies and persist with drab patterns like olives and Hare's Ear Czech Nymphs.

If, however, the water is coloured it will usually pay to cover the water with a team of Gold Heads and/or larger and brighter patterns.

I really do recommend that you go out and give this method a try. It makes an interesting change from spending a day on a small stillwater. Grayling are beautiful fish and are extremely rewarding to catch from a wild river. I would urge anybody tempted to go and give it a try!

Desert Island *flies*

Mickey Bewick's a fishing pioneer and a well-known face on the competition scene. So which three flies could he not live without?

CLARET HOPPER

This hopper can work all year round, but is especially effective when buzzers are hatching – from roughly the middle of May onwards.
It is usually fished static, cast towards rising trout but it can be also be tied on a heavier-gauge hook and used as a pulling pattern.
It really is my number-one choice for the top dropper position when fishing 'washing-line' style up on the surface.
You'll notice that the claret colour is lighter than usual – it comes from Ireland where it works really well – and is the same colour that many buzzers change to for a few seconds just before they are about hatch. Make a point of having the legs facing downwards, always!
The legs on Hopper patterns tend to be different, I find tying them this way is the most effective.

Hook: B170, size 12 to 10; B175 for pulling fly **Thread:** Brown **Body:** Medium claret seal's fur **Legs:** Knotted pheasant tail, two each side **Hackle:** Three to four turns of red game cock

DIAWL BACH

This is my standard Diawl Bach for clear-water conditions. I only carry two other variations – one with a holographic rib and another with a hot-orange head for when the water is dirty. There are literally thousands of variations of this pattern, but I don't see it as necessary to carry too many because my three patterns catch consistently all year round.
Once the water warms up, I use it to represent buzzers but it's a versatile pattern and it can be seen as many different types of nymphs.
I also works equally well for wild fish as well as stocked fish.
The lighter honey cock feather fibres used in this Diawl Bach represents a shuck perfectly and because of this I feel that it produces more takes for me than the standard brown tail and hackle.

Hook: B175, size 14 to 10 **Thread:** Brown **Tail:** Honey cock fibres **Rib:** Fine copper wire **Body:** Bronze peacock herl **Throat hackle:** Honey cock fibres **Cheeks:** Bronze peacock herl

CORMORANT BOOBY

It's an essential fly for fishing the 'washing-line' and is one of my favourite patterns at the moment. The key to its success is its natural colouration – it catches really well and has won some important competitions for me. So many anglers have boxes of eye-burningly bright lures that get stripped back as fast as possible because they look like nothing on earth. While this may catch some stockies, I'm sure it scares most other fish to death! My Booby's naturally coloured materials encourage wary fish to take, and it works well if used with a slow retrieve. It's the perfect partner for my other two flies featured here. I use green and natural jungle cock for the cheeks, but find that goose biots work just as well, and at a fraction of the price.

Hook: B175, size 12 to 10 **Thread:** Black **Tail:** Black marabou **Rib:** Fine copper **Body:** Bronze peacock herl **Wing:** Black marabou **Cheeks:** Green jungle cock **Eyes:** Black Plastozote

 ... the people · the performance · the passion

At **G.Loomis** we combine the world's most advanced carbon technology* with angling passion, technical experience and the world's most technologically advanced machines: Human hands.

The result? Well it just doesn't get any better.

WWW.GLOOMIS.COM

For a full list of Pro Shop stockists visit the G Loomis website.
All photos in this advert were taken at the G Loomis factory in Woodland USA. The only place where G Loomis rods are made.

Make Them Want *it*

Tim Smith says we shouldn't give salmon an easy time…
and shows how to stir them up into being unable to refuse.

e lot are far too polite when it comes to fishing for salmon. Now, I don't mean in letting fellow anglers down a pool first… or not using bad language on the riverbank.

I mean 'polite' when it comes to fishing our salmon flies. We cast at 45 degrees across the river and let it swing. We cast more squarely across in slower currents, and at a shallower angle in faster currents.

Okay, but that's about where politeness ends; with the fly swinging ever so harmlessly across the river at a gentle pace. Sometimes it's no wonder we don't catch anything, because the fish must be bored to tears!

The trout guys have been stirring fish up for years, by tearing aggressive flies through the water with even more aggressive retrieves. And so, too, have those fishing Scandinavian rivers… for salmon. So, what am I talking about?

In short, it's a big fly moved quickly through the water right into the face of the fish. Intimidation, I suppose you could call it. Provoking a violent response by annoying the hell out of

them could be another description!

You see, this is often a tactic employed when very fresh salmon are likely to be in the river. It's also great for running fish, especially in fast water.

Now salmon, when they first enter a river from the sea they tend to behave unpredictably. They have entered a new environment, they are keen to get on with the job of migrating to the river's upper reaches and they get twitchy and impatient.

How do you get an irritated person to snap? You wind them up! It's the same with Atlantic salmon, so try fishing aggressively!

RIVER CONDITIONS

This fishing style can be effective in a wide variety of conditions, but in fast and shallow water it really excels.

Many top ghillies all over the UK swear by the technique – even as early as February when everyone is fishing tubes slowly and deeply. Many other friends have used it successfully in high summer when the river at first

seems lifeless.

In times of low water, many people use this solely as a last-chance technique, when all else has failed. Having said that, it is often the favourite technique in other anglers' armouries!

It's all about confidence at the end of the day and, as a good friend once said to me: "If it's a great, when-all-else-fails technique why not use it all the time?"

KIT FOR THE JOB

Match your rod to the river you are fishing and to the size of fish you are likely to encounter, as you would when 'traditional' salmon fishing. Your normal lines will work, but if you are looking for an ideal set-up these techniques and flies are most effective used in conjunction with a short-headed Spey line or a shooting head. The short lines mean that you have to strip in running line before you

Shooting heads allow the most versatile approach when fishing these methods.

A square cast across the river will make the fly fish faster.

Long strips help race the fly across the current.

PROOF OF THE PUDDING

Right, I'm going to be totally honest here. The sequence of photographs below was shot on the River Laune in County Kerry, when Steve Cullen and I had two hours before flying back to Birmingham.

With it being the stretch of water I captured my first fly-caught salmon on many years ago, I really wanted to fish it. The locals told us there were very few fish around and that they were running straight through to the upper reaches.

After the two hours were up and not having seen one sign of a fish, we decided to take a short sequence of pictures on fishing the style of fly described above. Within about 10 minutes, we had the photographs of the fly, shooting head, square cast and strip retrieve. As the fly swung quickly in the tail of the pool, I turned to Steve to discuss other pictures.

You can guess what happened next, can't you? Yes, the flukiest moment in my salmon fishing career, beaching a sea-liced eight-pounder! It goes to show that the method really does work!

recast, ideal really because stripping line is often vital for fishing these flies effectively! In the same vein, when fishing small rivers a single-handed 8-wt set-up allows you to do this with ease.

So, to 'dig' the fly into the current before you start stripping line or swinging the fly, an intermediate or sink-tip line is perfect.

The flies can at times be effective when fished on a full floater, where a slight wake caused by the fast-moving fly on the surface can prove irresistible to salmon.

Hook-ups in these situations can be hard to secure, with fish hitting the fly seemingly out of pure frustration!

As far as leaders go, use either a heavy (30lb to 50lb) mono butt section (four to six feet) or a heavy tapered leader. Add your tippet (six feet or so), with breaking strain to suit the size of fish. Using tapered leaders will help turn these large flies over more effectively and should avoid it all landing in a heap.

RACING TECHNIQUES

Do everything faster. This is the simplest suggestion I can give you when it comes to really messing about with heads of salmon. You would normally cast at a shallow angle and swing the fly slowly in fast water; try casting square across the river.

In the gently flowing bellies of pools, try a square or even an upstream cast using long strips to race the fly around in a large arc. If you've ever fished lures on stillwaters you'll know the kind of effect to go for. Aggressive retrieves will often bring aggressive responses from fish. It may be exhausting at times to fish in this way, but it keeps you busy!

Another proven method in slow water is to back up the pool, making sure that no-one is intending to fish down behind you and making a square cast across the river.

Holding your rod at right angles to the current, walk upstream. This makes the fly swing smoothly and swiftly around in an arc and can provoke a violent response from the fish.

A fresh Laune salmon takes Tim by surprise…

The techniques described here are great in fast water.

… and while it is beached eventually, it isn't at all happy about it!

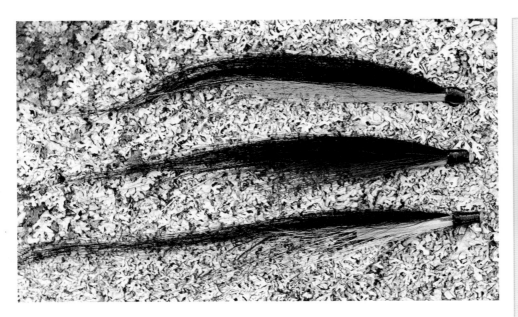

THE FLIES THAT MADE THEM HAVE IT

There are a number of patterns used regularly for this style of fishing. In general, they are dressed on lightweight (plastic or aluminium) tubes with long (4in to 10in) black wings made of goat, Icelandic horse, long fox or similar hair.

Think of Collie Dogs, extra-long Tempeldogs and the Sunray Shadow. It is often said that these patterns 'imitate' sandeels, a salmon food source at sea, but I don't think we will ever know for sure why salmon take them!

THE LEGENDARY BROOKS' SUNRAY SHADOW

There is arguably one fly – or family of flies – that is ideally suited to this style of fishing. Invented in the 1970s by the late Ray Brooks on Norway's

Lærdal River, the Brooks' Sunray Shadow is considered by many as being the greatest fast-water salmon fly.

The original, born out of Ray's years of experimentation on the Lærdal's glacial torrents, featured a brown underwing. In high water a white underwing was preferred and, in bright sunlight, a blue underwing.

Possibly the most interesting fact about the Brooks' Sunray Shadow is that it is patented! As such, unauthorised reproduction of the fly is strictly prohibited. So, unfortunately, we cannot give any details of how the fly is dressed… we're not even allowed to tie them!

(Note: Thanks to Paddy Bonner for the details and photograph.)

COLLIE DOG VARIANT

This is a version of the classic 'when-all-else-fails' pattern. Quite possibly the simplest salmon fly of them all, it has tempted countless salmon worldwide.

Tube: Aluminium or plastic, 1in to 1½in
Underwing: White buck tail
Wing: Black goat

BLACK AND GREEN TEMPELDOG

This should give you an idea about the length of the fly; this particular one is around six inches long! Black and green is a classic colour combination for Norwegian rivers but, for the UK, try tying this with a white or brown underwing instead of green.

Tube: Silver Loop Bottle, or 1in plastic or aluminium **Wing 1:** Bright-green Glo-Brite yarn **Wing 2:** Pearl Krystal Flash **Wing 3:** Green arctic fox **Wing 4:** Black or peacock Krystal Flash **Wing 5:** Black arctic fox **Hackle 1:** Green cock hackle **Hackle 2:** Black hen hackle **Cheeks:** Jungle cock

BLACK EXPERIMENT

One from innovative fly tyer Gary Champion, the cone on the front of this tube makes the fly wobble violently from side to side, further enhancing the aggressive movement of the fly when fished fast. It's a pain to cast, but it certainly does the damage!

Tube: Yuri Shumakov tubes (Firefly) **Head:** Marc Petitjean Magic Head, R13 **Wing 1:** White arctic fox **Wing 2:** Pearl Mirror Flash or Krystal Flash **Wing 3:** Black arctic fox **Hackle:** White cock **Cheeks:** Jungle cock